42

Shanghai

Select

contents

Shanghai overview

Time is turning full circle in Shanghai. Back in the roaring 1920s and '30s, the 'Pearl of the Orient' was one of the globe's most fashionable and talked-about cities. An economic boom had fuelled constructive creativity and a thriving nightlife scene fast became world famous. Fast-forward 80 years, and much the same is happening again.

China's most progressive, western-facing city is benefitting big time from globalisation. Pudong, on the east bank, little more than wasteland until the early 1990s, now looks like the set of a sci-fi film. Neon-glowing elevated highways seem to fly through the air, and the rocket-like Oriental Pearl Tower pierces the sky against the canyon of glittering skyscrapers framing Lujiazui district in Pudong. But west of the river, glorious old Shanghai can still be found in the stunning neoclassical and Art Deco buildings along the Bund and in

the architecture left behind in the old Concessions and in the Chinese *longtang* (lane) neighbourhoods.

In this spirited city of 21 million people tea stores, dim sum kiosks and Buddhist temples sit alongside contemporary art galleries, franchised coffee shops and BMW showrooms. The Shanghainese are savvy shoppers, and the city centre is saturated with glitzy malls and brand boutiques. At the same time, you can also find traditional offerings, such as bespoke tailoring, hand-painted porcelain, premium pearls and herbal remedies. After working or shopping, city dwellers like to kick back with a foot or body massage in one of the numerous spas and massage parlours citywide.

Shanghai's nightlife and dining scene is fast challenging Hong Kong and Singapore. The best ways to enjoy the city's after-dark splendour include strolling along the riverside Bund or sipping a cocktail in one of several sky-high cocktail lounges.

Street signs are in English and Chinese, and English is increasingly understood in the main neighbourhoods (though not by taxi drivers!). The extensive metro system is modern, efficient and cheap, and Shanghai is a very safe city day and night – so go explore.

in the mood for...

... street life

Shanghai life is lived on the streets. Vibrant French Concession boulevards like **Fuxing Road West** *(p.94)* and **Shaanxi Road South** *(p.112)* blend heritage architecture with back-to-back shops and day-night street theatre. Equally absorbing is **Dongtai Road** *(p.57)*, where antique dealers vie for business with souvenir shops, and the food market on nearby **Fangbang Road** *(p.65)* – a hive of activity after dark.

... 1930s glamour

Nowhere evokes the glamour of 1930s Shanghai more than the iconic **Peace Hotel** *(p.28)* whose splendid Art Deco interiors have been revamped and reopened. A drink at **Yongfoo Elite** *(p.98)*, a fabulous Concession-era villa chockful of period antiques, will transport you back in time, as will a tea dance to gentle jazz tunes at the **Paramount Theatre** ballroom *(p.81)* which remains a Shanghai institution. Revive the glamorous 'Paris of the Orient' look with a figure-hugging *qipao* dress by **Jane Zhu** and a pair of silk slippers from **Suzhou Cobblers** *(p.34)*.

... fine dining

Whereas fine dining was once restricted to deluxe hotels, high-quality Chinese and international cuisines are now offered across a city with an avowed ambition to be recognised globally as a dining destination. Nowhere sates modern Shanghai's penchant for see-and-be-seen dining and riverside terrace views better than **M on the Bund**. Across the road, celebrity chef Jean Georges Vongerichten serves haute French at **Three on the Bund**, while inventive European cuisine is on the menu at French chef Paul Pairet's **Mr & Mrs Bund**. The elegant dining room of **Yi Long Court** serves delicious modern Cantonese cooking by a Michelin-starred chef from Hong Kong (*all above p.32*). Australian-Greek chef David Laris offers an intimate 8- or 12-course feast for a dozen diners at **12 Chairs** (*p.95*). Above-mentioned Paul Pairet threatens to upstage him with his latest venture, **Ultraviolet** (*p.149*) which serves a choreographed 20-course 'molecular' menu to just 10 diners. **Fu 1088**, (*p.163*) meanwhile, serves classic and experimental Chinese dishes in a lavishly decorated villa.

... retail therapy

Retail revenues are emerging as a key driver of the local economy, and shopping is an acknowledged obsession with the newly affluent class. Today's consumers are increasingly spoilt for choice. Premium purchasing is offered in the glassy malls that stretch along **Huaihai Road** and **Nanjing Road West** (*p.82*), while the narrow lanes of **Xintiandi** (*p.52*) attract a boutique brand clientele to shop, lunch and ostentatiously sip coffees on outdoor terraces. Young Shanghai fashion designers showcase their latest couture, jewellery and accessory lines in restored houses and factories clustered around **Taikang Road** (*p.96*). The uber-glam flagships of **The Bund** (*p.34*) provide sedate shopping with superior views, while on the opposite bank of the Huangpu River, the **Shanghai IFC** mall (*p.125*) in Pudong is a smart destination for label-led shoppers.

Specialist shops and markets abound. Lustrous gem-quality pearls can be found at **Hangqiao Pearl City** (*p.159*); **Tianshan Tea City** (*p.157*) is a three-storey emporium of fine tea; a dazzling array of silks, cashmeres and linens are on display at the **South Bund Fabric Market** (*p.58*); the **Dongtai Road Antiques Market** (*p.57*) is a chaotic mixture of genuine antiques and pure kitsch. The small shops in the **Yu Garden Bazaar** specialising in kites, canes, knives, buttons, chopsticks and fans are a sight to behold (*p.54*).

... romance

Noisy and brash as it can be, Shanghai knows how to set a romantic mood. Share a petal-strewn bath at the **Bund Five Spa Oasis** *(p.37)*, followed by a decadent afternoon tea at the **Peninsula Hotel** *(p.173)*. Or take a tandem ride through the leafy lanes of the French Concession *(p.103)*, then dine *à deux* on exotic Yunnanese dishes in the moodily lit **Lost Heaven** *(pictured; p.63)*. To round off your day, whisk your loved one up to the **VUE** bar terrace, cuddle up on a daybed with a glass of bubbly, and take in the dreamy views *(p.150)*.

... escaping the crowds

Thankfully in this seething metropolis, peaceful retreats abound. Little **Jing An Park** in the heart of Shanghai is a fine spot for a stroll and some people-watching *(p.78)*. Set amid fragrant osmanthus trees, the pavilion teahouse of **Guilin Park** *(p.168)* ranks high as a Zen-infused respite. A contemplative walk around nearby **Longhua Martyrs Memorial** *(p.165)* takes in commemorative statues within a lovely manicured park. To escape Xujiahui's relentless commercial buzz, just duck inside the splendid **St Ignatius Cathedral** *(p.167)*.

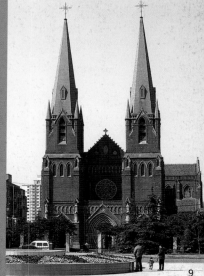

... a night on the town

Shanghai's notoriously decadent 1930s nightlife scene entered a prolonged lull following World War II and the 1949 Communist Revolution. Half a century later, in the early Noughties, bar and club culture entered a kind of Baby Boomer explosion – mirroring China's economic boom. Today,

Shanghai's nightlife compares favourably with any hard-partying Asian metropolis.

Opened early in the new century, Xintiandi is a labyrinth of upscale bars and restaurants, where menu prices are largely tailored for credit card-carrying tourists. In 2010, **Sinan Mansions** *(p.95)* emerged as Xintiandi's

more street savvy competitor. A clutch of revamped 1930s mansions, it is home to some of Shanghai's most popular bars and diners. The elegant French Concession streets are dotted with casual-cool drinking spots, notably **The Apartment** and **El Coctel** on Yongfu Road *(p.98)*, and **Dr Wine** on Fumin Road.

For stylish cocktail lounges with a terrace view, the elegant riverside **Bund** is suitably well endowed. **Glamour Bar** *(p.36)*, **New Heights** *(p.33)*, **Bar Rouge** *(p.35)* and **Char** *(p.175)* at Hotel Indigo are the top picks, while updated retro Shanghai chic is served up at the **Long Bar** *(p.29)* inside the neoclassical Waldorf Astoria hotel.

Across the Huangpu River in Pudong, movers and shakers ascend to **Flair**, an alfresco lounge that affords dramatic skyline panoramas from the 58th floor of the Shanghai IFC Tower *(p.122)*.

Back down to earth, live music in Shanghai tends to be of the more soulful variety; talented musicians and vocalists from home and abroad grace the stages most nights at **House of Blues and Jazz** *(p.35)* and **JZ Club** *(p.105)*. Weekend party people make for **M1NT** and hip Hong Kong club export **Drop** *(p.35)*.

Those more classically inclined are well served by two stunning world-class venues, the **Shanghai Grand Theatre** *(p.73)* and **Shanghai Oriental Arts Centre** *(p.131)*.

... family fun

A reputation for daytime consumerism and after-dark excess suggests Shanghai is not a family destination. Like everything in this constantly evolving metropolis, though, attractions for young travellers are increasingly springing up. A popular starting point is the indoor ice rink at the **Mercedes-Benz Arena** *(p.133)* in Pudong, followed by a visit to the **China Pavilion** *(p.127)* at the 2010 World Expo Site, which really does look like it was made of Lego. Also east of the river is the adult-sounding but very kid-friendly **Shanghai Science and Technology Museum** *(p.133)* which overlooks **Century Park** *(p.130)* – a popular spot for kite flying, rollerblading and Frisbee throwing at weekends. Located by the Pudong waterside is the **Shanghai Ocean Aquarium** *(p.133)* where sharks, Chinese water dragons and jellyfish hold youngsters in thrall.

Head to the **Bund Sightseeing Tunnel** *(p.31)* for a kaleidoscopic, visually stimulating train ride beneath the Huangpu River. Also universally loved by children is taking the high-speed lift up the **Oriental Pearl Tower** *(p.128)*.

... historic architecture

After Shanghai was forcibly opened up as an international port following the 1840–42 Sino-British Opium War, foreign developers set to work. The constructive legacy of 19th- and early 20th-century British, French and American domination is evident citywide. Most evocative are the neoclassical mansions of the **Bund** (*p.26*) which hug the arcing western bank of the Huangpu River.

Head inland and **People's Square** – originally a British-built racecourse – is flanked by a handful of Art Deco gems, including some historic hotels (*p.75*). The former **French Concession** (*p.94, p.108*) is an alluring mix of soulful architecture, ranging from Art Deco apartment residences to European villas and manor houses – many of which have been converted into bars, restaurants and boutique hotels.

North of People's Square, **Hongkou** is another district richly imbued with historic architecture, including the World War II **Jewish Ghetto** (*p.139*) and **1933** (*p.140*), an Art Deco abattoir turned retail and dining destination. More surprising landmarks can be admired on the **North Bank of Suzhou Creek**, just across **Waibaidu Bridge**, itself an architectural icon (*p.144*).

in the mood for...

... modern icons

Shanghai's name translates into English as 'Above the Sea', and staring at the cloud-level skyline, elevation is the dominant theme – especially east of the river in Pudong. Here, the fast-rising **Shanghai Tower** will, in 2014, shoot higher than the **Shanghai World Financial Centre** and the **Jinmao Tower** – two of Asia's tallest buildings *(p.120)*. Modern architecture blending western function and Asian influences, include architect Arata Isozaki's **Himalayas Centre** *(p.129)* and the Paul Andreu-designed **Oriental Art Centre** *(p.131)*, while the **China Pavilion** *(p.127)* at the 2010 World Expo site is a contemporary take on traditional Chinese structural design. Coming out of left-field is the oyster shell-shaped **Mercedes-Benz Arena** *(p.131)* which resembles a spaceship about to take off when lit in neon at night. In Puxi, two ultra high-rise towers containing the **JW Marriott Tomorrow Square** and **Le Royal Meridien Shanghai** *(p.178)* dominate the 1930s Art Deco gems on People's Square. Here, too, modern architecture makes its mark in the form of the **Shanghai Grand Theatre** *(p.73)* and the **Urban Planning Exhibition Centre** *(p.72)*.

... contemporary art

Chinese contemporary art has become one of the hottest commodities in the art world and Shanghai has cleverly combined culture with commerce to become a major art centre. A cluster of former industrial buildings on **Moganshan Road** have been transformed into the city's premier art district where leading galleries show works by China's top artists (*p.142*). West of the city centre, **Redtown** (*p.161*) features sculpture, painting and photographic galleries set around a park. A concentration of small galleries can be found in the lanes of the former French Concession including the independent and internationally minded **Art Labor** (*p.113*). North of downtown, **ShangArt Taopu** (*p.143*) is a relatively new arts centre and studio complex in a once-derelict factory. Even further afield in Baoshan, the superbly curated **Shanghai Museum of Glass** (*p.141*) more than merits the journey.

More central art venues include the **Rockbund Art Museum** (*p.30*) in a renovated 1930s building behind the Bund, and **Shanghai MOCA** (*p.70*) in the heart of People's Park. In Pudong, the new **Himalayas Art Museum** (*p.129*) forms part of the Himalayas Centre, which focuses on Chinese culture and performing arts.

... being pampered

Shanghai's high-octane moneymakers and office toilers rebalance their inner calm with a relaxing back or foot rub. As a result, most streets feature a (legal) massage parlour and/or a full-service urban spa. Locally based mid-range spa chain **Dragonfly** (p.124) has multiple branches offering Chinese and aroma massages and facials. Styled with Cambodian motifs and wall reliefs, **Apsara Spa** (p.76) specialises in decadent body treatments from Indochina. Asia's first **Evian Spa** (p.37) at Three on the Bund blends Eastern and European therapies and beauty treatments – ranging from a colour hydrotherapy massage to a Dead Sea Mud Mask or revitalising eye contour treatment. For the ultimate wellness high, take the elevator to the 53rd floor of Pudong's IFC Shanghai tower. Here, the **Ritz-Carlton Spa by ESPA** (p.173) is a sumptuous sky-high retreat offering Swedish and aromatherapy massage, facial scrubs and body wraps, a specialist men's treatment menu and an infinity swimming pool yielding dramatic city panoramas.

... local cuisine

Shanghai reads like a culinary map of the nation. For delicious *xiaolongbao* dumplings, try Taiwanese chain **Din Tai Fung** *(p.126)*. **Sichuan Citizen** *(p.106)* serves up peppery hotpots from the mountainous southwest, while **Lost Heaven** *(p.63)* fuses Yunnan, Thai and Burmese flavours. For fresh Shanghai street food, follow your nose to the **Fangbang Road Food Market** *(p.65)*. For a sizzling Korean barbecue hotfoot it to **Ben Jia** *(p.162)* in Hongqiao. And for classic wood-fired Beijing Duck, **Xindalu** *(p.176)* at the Hyatt on the Bund hotel is hard to beat.

... literary inspiration

During its 1930s heyday, Shanghai was the heart of China's literary scene, and it remains an important centre even with today's heavily censured media. North of downtown, **Duolun Road** *(p.138)* has many restored houses and cafés frequented by Shanghai's pre-War literati. At the quaint **Old China Hand Reading Room** *(p.102)* you can browse fascinating tomes while sipping tea. Host venue for the annual Shanghai International Literary Festival, **Glamour Bar** *(p.36)* also presents Sunday afternoon talks by visiting authors year-round.

neighbourhoods

The limits of this maritime city are defined by its waterways. The Huangpu River separates Shanghai's newest district, Pudong in the east, from the rest of Shanghai, or rather Puxi, to the west. The Suzhou Creek divides the thriving midsection of Puxi from its quieter northern suburbs. New lines have been drawn, but the shape and feel of the old foreign Concessions and Nanshi – the Old Chinese City – are still discernible. Shanghai streets run north to south and east to west in grid-like fashion, except for oval-shaped Nanshi and People's Square, the latter defined by the old racetracks.

The Bund and Huangpu Shanghai's most celebrated strip of historic real estate is the Bund, which stretches for one mile along the west bank of the Huangpu River. Here, stately colonial-era buildings have been converted into hotels, restaurants, banks and boutiques. The intriguing streets and lanes behind the Bund are filled with fine architecture and the enduring aura of Old Shanghai.

Xintiandi, Yu Garden and South Bund Southwest of the Bund, Xintiandi (meaning 'New Heaven and Earth') is a two-block area of refurbished *shikumen* or lane houses, filled with boutiques, restaurants and bars. To the east, this buzzing shopping and nightlife enclave segues via the Dongtai Antique Market into Nanshi – the Old Chinese City around Yu Garden – and the South Bund.

People's Square and Jing'an The People's Square area is the city's geographical centre, its oval shape delineated by the former British-built racetrack. The old Jockey Club is now the Shanghai Museum of Art, while thought-provoking contemporary landmarks including the Urban Planning Exhibition Hall, Shanghai Grand Theatre and leafy People's Park are part of a hotchpotch landscape framed by soaring mega-towers. Shanghai's main metro lines all converge at this town square, transporting people from all over the city to its cultural and political hub.

French Concession In the mid-19th century, Shanghai was carved into self-governing 'concessions' by the invading British, American and French powers. The French Concession south of what is today's Yan'an Elevated Highway became the city's most architecturally rich district, with European villas, Art Deco residences and plane trees flanking the French-named avenues. Today, these elegant streets boast some of Shanghai's most charming restaurants, cafés and drinking spots.

Pudong Until the 1990s, the vast tract of land east of the Huangpu River was a sparsely populated area of marshland. Fast-forward to today, and Pudong epitomises future Shanghai. The riverside Lujiazui district is home to China's financial centre, one of its two stock exchanges and its tallest skyscrapers. Beyond is a sprawling residential and retail landscape of high-rise hotels, glitzy malls and China's second-busiest airport.

Suzhou Creek and the Northern Districts North of People's Square, are the rapidly gentrifying districts around Suzhou Creek. Former factories and warehouses of this old industrial zone are being converted into hip museums, galleries and artists' studios. The forgotten district around Jiangwan Stadium is an impressive legacy of attempts by Chiang Kai-shek's Nationalists to build a new city on Shanghai's fringes.

Xujiahui, Changning and Hongqiao These adjacent western districts span the thriving mall scene and historic attractions of Xujiahui, the high-rise hotels and high-speed railway hub of Hongqiao and the western extremity of the French Concession. Awaiting discovery is an eclectic mix of sculpture gardens, Japanese and Korean cuisine, a Gothic cathedral and an exquisitely landscaped park.

YICHUAN

YANGJIAQIAO

ZHENRU

ZHUJIAWAN

MENGQING
GONGYUAN

Shanghai Huochezhan
(Shanghai Railway Station)

M50

CHANGSHOU
GONGYUAN

Yu Fo Si
(Jade Buddha Temple)

JING AN

Suzhou C

Xin

WUSONG

RENMIN GON
(PEOPLE'S P

Shanghai Renmin Zhengfu
(City Hall)

Shanghai
Shangcheng
(Shanghai Centre)

Shanghai Bowugu
(Shanghai Muse

ZHONGSHAN
GONGYUAN

Jingan Si
(Jing An Temple)

Shanghai Zhanlan
Zhongxin
(Shanghai
Exhibition Centre)

Shang Xi

Shi Shaonian Gong
(Municipal Children's Palace/Marble Hall)

JINGAN
GONGYUAN

XIANGYANG
GONGYUAN

Xint

ZHOUJIAQIAO

FUXING
GONGYUAN

TAIPI
GON

Sun Zhongsh
(former Reside
Sun Yat-sen)

Zhongguo Lanyin
Huabu Guan
(Chinese Printed Blue
Nankeen Exhibition Hall)

DINGXIANG
HUAYUAN

FRENCH
CONCESSION

Wenhua Guangchang
(Cultural Square)

Zhou Enlai G
(former reside
Zhou Enlai)

Mary Ching
& Leo Gallery

Shanghai Tushuguan
(Shanghai Library)

Jiashan
Market

Tianzifang

HONGQIAO

CHANGNING

Guojie Jiaotang
(Shanghai
International
Community Church)

Hongqiao International Airport

Zhongguo Gongchandang
Shanghai Shi Wei Yuanhui
(Communist Party HQ)

XUJIAHUI
GONGYUAN

DAPUQIAO

Soong Qingling's
Mausoleum

Bibliotheca
Zikawei

Nanpu
Railway
Station

Dapu R
Tu

XUHUI

MINHANG

Shanghai Botanical Garden

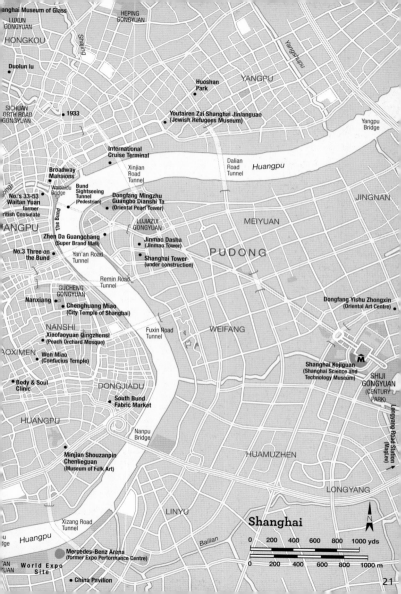

Shanghai Museum of Glass

HEPING GONGYUAN

LUXUN GONGYUAN

HONGKOU

Shajing

Duolun lu

SICHUAN NORTH ROAD GONGYUAN

1933

Huoshan Park

YANGPU

Yangpu

Youtairen Zai Shanghai Jinianguan (Jewish Refugees Museum)

Yangpu Bridge

International Cruise Terminal

Xinjian Road Tunnel

Dalian Road Tunnel

Huangpu

Broadway Mansions

Waibaidu Bridge

Bund Sightseeing Tunnel (Pedestrian)

Dongfang Mingzhu Guangbo Dianshi Ta (Oriental Pearl Tower)

JINGNAN

No.'s 33-53 Waitan Yuan former British Consulate

The Bund

LUJIAZUI GONGYUAN

MEIYUAN

WANGPU

Zhen Da Guangchang (Super Brand Mall)

Jinmao Dasha (Jinmao Tower)

PUDONG

Yan'an Road Tunnel

Shanghai Tower (under construction)

No.3 Three on the Bund

Remin Road Tunnel

JIJCHENG GONGYUAN

Dongfang Yishu Zhongxin (Oriental Art Centre)

Nanxiang

Chenghuang Miao (City Temple of Shanghai)

NANSHI

WEIFANG

Xiaofaoyuan Qingzhensi (Peach Orchard Mosque)

Fuxin Road Tunnel

AOXIMEN

Wen Miao (Confucius Temple)

M

Body & Soul Clinic

Shanghai Kejiguan (Shanghai Science and Technology Museum)

SHIJI GONGYUAN (CENTURY PARK)

DONGJIADU

South Bund Fabric Market

Longyang Road Station (Maglev)

HUANGPU

Nanpu Bridge

Minjian Shouzanpin Chenlieguan (Museum of Folk Art)

HUAMUZHEN

LONGYANG

LINYU

Xizang Road Tunnel

Shanghai

Bailian

0   200   400   600   800   1000 yds

0   200   400   600   800   1000 m

N

Huangpu

...dge

Mercedes-Benz Arena (former Expo Performance Centre)

World Expo Site

...'AN

China Pavilion

21

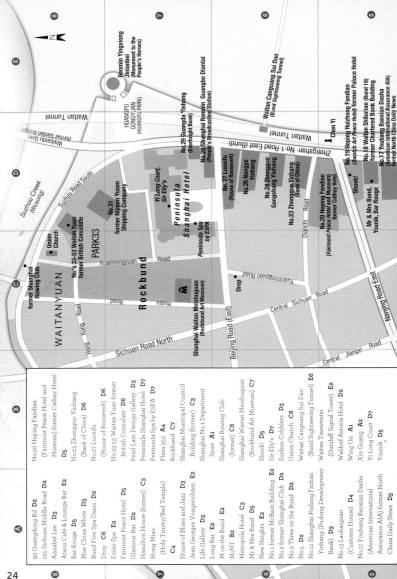

Map labels

WAITANYUAN

Rockbund

PARK33

Suzhou Creek (Wusong)

Walbaidu Qiao (former Garden Bridge)

Waitan Tunnel

HUANGPU GONGYUAN (HUANGPU PARK)

Renmin Yingxiong Jinianbei (Monument to the People's Heroes)

former Shanghai Rowing Club

Union Church

No.5's 33–53 Waitan Yuan former British Consulate

No.31 former Nippon Yusen Shipping Company

Yi Long Court, Sir Elly's

Peninsula Shanghai Hotel

Peninsula Spa by ESPA

Yuanmingyuan Road

Hubin Road

Hong Kong Road

Sichuan Road North

Beijing Road (East)

Central Sichuan Road

Shanghai Waitan Meishuguan (Rockbund Art Museum)

Drop

Yuanmingyuan Road

Dianchi Road

Zhongshan No.1 Road East (Bund)

No.29 Guangda Yinhang (Everbright Bank)

No.28 Shanghai Renmin Guangbo Diantai (People's Broadcasting Station)

No.27 Luosifu (House of Roosevelt)

No.26 Hongye Yinhang

No.24 Zhongguo Gongshang Yinhang

No.23 Zhongguo Yinhang (Bank of China)

No.20 Heping Fandian (Fairmont Peace Hotel and Museum) former Cathay Hotel

No.19 Heping Huizhong Fandian (Swatch Art Peace Hotel) former Palace Hotel

No.18 Waitan Shibahao (Bund 18) former Chartered Bank Building

No.17 Youbang Baoxian Dasha (American International Assurance AIA) former North China Daily News

Chen Yi

Shook!

Mr & Mrs Bund, Younik, Bar Rouge

Waitan Canguang Sui Dao (Bund Sightseeing Tunnel)

Suzhou Road South

Suzhou Road South

Nanjing Road East

Central Jiangxi Road

Index list

93 Guangdong Rd **D2**

125 Sichuan Middle Road **D2**

Annabel Lee **E2**

Atanu Café & Lounge Bar **E2**

Bar Rouge **D5**

Blue China White **D3**

Bund Five Spa Oasis **D2**

Drop **C6**

Evian Spa **E2**

Fairmont Peace Hotel **D5**

Glamour Bar **D2**

Hamilton House (former) **C3**

Hong Miao (Holy Trinity/Red Temple) **C4**

House of Blues and Jazz **D3**

Jean Georges Vongerichten **E2**

Life Gallery **D3**

Long Bar **E2**

M on the Bund **E2**

M1NT **B2**

Metropole Hotel **C3**

Mr & Mrs Bund **D5**

New Heights **E2**

No.1 former McBain Building **E2**

No.2 former Shanghai Club **D2**

No.3 Three on the Bund **D2**

No.5 **D5**

No.12 Shanghai Pudong Fazhan Yinhang (Pudong Development Bank) **D3**

No.13 Laohaiguan (Customs House) **D4**

No.17 Youbang Baoxian Dasha (American International Assurance AIA) former North China Daily News **D5**

No.20 Heping Fandian (Fairmont Peace Hotel and Museum) former Cathay Hotel **D5**

No.23 Zhongguo Yinhang (Bank of China) **D6**

No.27 Luosifu (House of Roosevelt) **D6**

No.33-53 Waitan Yuan former British Consulate **D8**

Pearl Lam Design Gallery **D3**

Peninsula Shanghai Hotel **D7**

Peninsula Spa by ESPA **D7**

Plaza 353 **A4**

Rockbund **C7**

Shanghai Municipal Council Building (former) **C3**

Shanghai No.1 Department Store **A1**

Shanghai Rowing Club (former) **A1**

Shanghai Waitan Meishuguan (Rockbund Art Museum) **C7**

Shook! **D5**

Sir Elly's **D7**

Suzhou Cobblers **C8**

Union Church **C8**

Waitan Canguang Sui Dao (Bund Sightseeing Tunnel) **E6**

Waitan Tianwentai (Gutzlaff Signal Tower) **E2**

Waldorf Astoria Hotel **D2**

Wing On **A1**

Xin Guang **A2**

Yi Long Court **D7**

Younik **D5**

The Bund and Huangpu

angpu

黄浦区

Promenade

Waitan Tunnel

Zhongshan No.1 Road East (Bund)

former Russo-Asiatic Bank

No.14

No.13 Laohaiguan (Customs House)

No.12 Shanghai Pudong Fazhan Yinhang (Pudong Development Bank)

No.17 former Russell & Company

Blue China White, Suzhou Cobblers, Annabel Lee and Life Gallery

No.7 Bangkok Bank

No.6

No.5

M on the Bund, Glamour Bar & Bund Five Spa Oasis

Jean Georges Vongerichten, Evian Spa and New Heights'

No.3, Three on the Bund

Long Bar

Waldorf Astoria (No.2 former Shanghai Club)

No.1 former McBain Building

Atanu Café & Lounge Bar

Waitan Tianwentai (Gutzlaff Signal Tower) (Bund Signal Tower)

Pearl Lam Design Gallery (185 Sichuan Middle Road)

House of Blues and Jazz

Central Sichuan Road

Xinhua News Group (125 Sichuan Middle Road)

China Minsheng Bank (93 Guangdong Road)

Guangdong Road

Metropole Hotel

former Hamilton House

Hongkou Road (Hankou Lu)

Jiujiang Road

Fuzhou Road

Central Jiangxi Road

former Shanghai Municipal Council Building

former American Club

Hong Miao (Holy Trinity / Red Temple)

Central Henan Road (Henan Zhong Lu)

Jiujiang Road (Jiujiang Lu)

Fuzhou Road

Central Shandong Road

MINT

Shanghai Ziran Bowuguan (Museum of Natural History)

Ⓜ

see above

Peninsula Shanghai Hotel

Zhongshan No.1 Road (E.) (Bund)

Beijing Donglu

Nanjing Road (E.)

Jiujiang Road

Hankou Road

Fuzhou Road

Central Jiangxi Road

Central Sichuan Road

Shanghai Ziran Bowuguan (Museum of Natural History)

Ⓜ

Yan'an Road East (Yan'an Dong Lu)

Henan Road

Central

Central

Central

Shandong Rd

Nanjing Road Pedestrian Mall

Plaza 353

Nanjing Road Pedestrian Mall

Niuzhuang Road

Beijing Road (E.)

Niuzhuang Road

Ningbo Road

Tianjin Road

Fujian

Guangxi Rd (N.)

Nanjing Road (E.)

Xin Guang

Wing On

Mo'en Tang (Moore Church)

Raffles City

Shanghai No.1 Department Store

Central

Guangxi Rd (N.)

Fuzhou Rd

Zhejiang

Guangdong Rd

Yan'an Road (E.)

Central Tibet (Xizang) Road

N

0   50   100   150   200 m
0   50   100   150   200 yds

0   500 m
0   500 yds

25

Take a **walking tour** of the iconic **Bund**, and admire the stately **colonial mansions** of Old Shanghai

Known locally as Waitan (Outside Beach), the two-kilometre sweep of magnificent historic buildings west of the Huangpu River, is a Concession-era time capsule. After the end of the first Sino-British Opium War in 1842, China was forced to open up Shanghai's port to foreign trade. What was then a muddy river bank became the docking station for merchant ships. As commerce boomed, this waterfront stretch became the economic engine of the British Concession. An embankment lined with jetties was built in the late 1880s, and by the early 20th century, the Bund (from the Anglo-Indian word meaning embanked quay), backed by trading houses and the grandiose headquarters of international financial institutions, had become known as the 'Wall Street of Asia'.

Almost a century later, Shanghai's riverfront was given a multi-million dollar makeover ahead of the 2010 World Expo. Traffic lanes were rerouted underground, the riverside boardwalk was broadened, new public spaces were created. and the iconic buildings were sandblasted and endowed with beautiful new lighting.

A WALK ALONG THE BUND
Starting at the southern end of the Bund, the first building is the neoclassical **McBain Building** (No.1), built in 1915.

Formerly the HQ of a shipping magnate, it is now used as offices. The elegant 1911 building at No.2, once occupied by the exclusive Shanghai club, is now the glitzy **Waldorf Astoria** (*p.29*). Next door, the former **Union Assurance Building** (No.3) is one of nine neoclassical buildings designed by British architects, Palmer & Turner. Now named **Three on the Bund**, it houses the gourmet temple of Jean Georges Vongerichten (*p.32*) among other restaurants and shops. At No.5, the former Nissin Kisen Kaisha Shipping Building, dating to 1925, is now occupied by Huaxia Bank, but its most famous contemporary tenants are the **M on the Bund** restaurant (*p.32*) and the cool **Glamour Bar** (*p.36*).

Heading up the Bund, you'll come to two of its most iconic buildings. The palatial **Shanghai Pudong Development Bank** (No. 12) was designed by Palmer & Turner as the HQ for the Hong Kong and Shanghai bank. When completed in 1921, it was hailed as 'the finest building east of the Suez'. Inside, the cavernous marble lobby features a cupola mosaic depicting images of the eight global cities in which the bank then operated. Opened in 1927, the neighbouring **Custom House**

(No. 13) is another Palmer & Turner gem. The bronze bas relief in the entrance lobby depicts heroic revolution symbolically set in front of the foreign-built Bund. The clock tower, fondly referred to as 'The Big Ching', was modelled on London's Big Ben. The American International Assurance or AIA building at No. 17 was the Bund's tallest when completed in 1923 as the **North China Daily News** HQ. The oldest and most influential newspaper of the time operated here from 1864 to 1951. The lobby is open during office hours so be sure to take a peek at its interior. Past the iconic **Peace Hotel** at No. 20 (*p.28*), the slim **Bank of China** (No. 22), another Palmer & Turner creation, is a harmonious blend of Chinese, classical and Art Deco themes (open during working hours). Built in 1922, the granite-clad **House of Roosevelt** at No. 27, formerly the Jardine Matheson building, was one of the great trading houses of Concession-era Shanghai. It is now a collection of bars, restaurants and shops.

The last buildings on the Bund are the oldest. Built in 1873 Nos. 33–53 were occupied by the former **British Consulate**. The buildings are off limits but the grounds are open to the public (*p.30*).

Saunter through the hallowed halls of the **Peace Hotel** and listen to its octogenarian **jazz band**

The Shanghai landscape owes considerable thanks to Sir Victor Sassoon. During the 1920s and '30s, the flamboyant financier and scion of the great opium-trading firm, E.D. Sassoon, built several of the city's finest buildings, including Hamilton House, Metropole Hotel, Cathay Cinema, Cathay Mansions and the Embankment Building. The tycoon's most prized legacy, however, is Sassoon House, known today as the **Fairmont Peace Hotel**. When it opened in 1929, Sassoon House incorporated the ultra-luxurious Cathay Hotel on its fourth to seventh floors. China's finest

hotel fast became a legend in a city of legends. From day one, the sleek, Art Deco building crowned by a green copper pyramid was the social centre of Shanghai. Business leaders, celebrities, gangsters and the social elite partied in the sprung wooden ballroom and luxuriated in hotel rooms with previously unseen luxuries such as air conditioning, Lalique glass detailing, marble bathrooms and silver coffee pots. Noel Coward, Charlie Chaplin and George Bernard Shaw all checked in during its heyday.

Following three years of much needed renovations, Shanghai's most iconic hotel reopened in 2010. The second-floor Peace Museum tells compelling stories, through photos and hotel artefacts, including serving spoons and crystal goblets engraved with the Cathay Hotel logo, of the 'Claridges of the East' and its benefactor.

For a musical meander down memory lane, the vintage jazz band (all members are aged 70+) still plays timeless tunes each evening in the **Jazz Bar**.

Fairmont Peace Hotel; 20 Nanjing Road East; tel: 6321 6888; www. fairmont.com/peacehotel; map D5

Prop up the **legendary Long Bar** and imbibe some **1930s glamour** at the Waldorf Astoria Shanghai

As a coastal city built on shipping wealth, Shanghai quickly developed a taste for waterside tippling. Few venues are more redolent of its formative drinking days than the old Shanghai Club.

Renowned in the 1920s and '30s as the most elitist social institution in Shanghai's International Concession, the Club was housed in a neoclassical Bund mansion fronted by dramatic arched windows and Corinthian columns. Inside, gentlemen of wealth and rank (it was out of bounds to everyone else) imbibed at the 33-metre (100ft) **Long Bar** and puffed Cuban cigars beneath humming ceiling fans.

The pre-War Japanese invasion of Shanghai shuttered the Club, but its legend lived on through the building's post-war days as the International Seamen's Club, a sleazy casino and China's first KFC branch.

In late 2010, the Shanghai Club legend was revived. Following three years of renovations, No.2 the Bund was reopened as the lavish Waldorf Astoria Shanghai on the Bund. Standing proud amid the hotel's Sicilian marble columns and patina marble floors, is the modern incarnation of the famed Long Bar.

Re-created using historic photos and architectural drawings, the Long Bar is outfitted with Jacobean wood panelling and backlit liquor cabinets. The replica bar – once the longest in Asia – features carved insignia and a white marble counter. Studded leather armchairs, Art Deco lamps, and sepia-tinted photos of Old Shanghai, complete the nostalgic picture.

So, do as the bank managers and taipans once did. Sink into an armchair, sip a Pink Gin and relax in one of Asia's most fabled drinking establishments.

The Long Bar; Waldorf Astoria Shanghai on the Bund, 2 Zhongshan No. 1 Road East; tel: 6322 9988; www. waldorfastoriashanghai.com; daily 2pm–1am; map D2

Peruse the born-again **Rockbund district**, stopping in at the Rockbund **Art Museum**

Waitanyuan – meaning 'headstream of the Bund' – lies behind the northern sweep of the Bund where Suzhou Creek meets the Huangpu River. This long-neglected historic area is in the process of a long-term urban renewal project under the guidance of British starchitect David Chipperfield. Due for completion in 2014, it will encompass luxury residences, offices, retail, hotels and museums.

The centerpiece of the six-acre Rockbund project is a clutch of heritage buildings between Yuanmingyuan Road and Huqiu Road, running parallel to the Bund. First to open was the **Rockbund Art Museum** in the revamped former Royal

Asiatic Society building dating from 1932. The six-floor Art Deco gallery hosts regular art, installation and photography exhibitions and has a cute café and terrace on the top floor.

A line of restored buildings strung along the newly pedestrianised Yuanmingyuan Road date from between 1924 and 1933. These eclectic facades feature bold Art Deco and neoclassical styling and unique Chinese influences.

Directly opposite are the grounds of the former British Consulate, accessible from the Bund side (ignore the severe looking guards – it is actually a public park). Although the residences, now private clubs and event venues, are off limits the gardens are delightful to stroll in and are home to several century-old trees. As you swing around to the main Bund promenade note the former **Shanghai Rowing Club** dating from 1904, offset by spectacular views of Art Deco monoliths on the opposite bank of Suzhou Creek (*p.144*).

Rockbund Art Museum; 20 Huqiu Road; tel: 3310 9985; www. rockbundartmuseum.org; Tue–Sun 10am–6pm; charge; map C7

Experience a trippy **underwater voyage** through the **Bund Sightseeing Tunnel**

There are a number of ways to cross the Huangpu River. The Bund Sightseeing Tunnel is undoubtedly the wackiest. The tunnel runs from beneath the promenade opposite No.27 on the Bund, exiting at the Oriental Pearl Tower on the Lujiazui bankside. The capsule ride takes passengers on a visual journey from the earth's molten core to outer space. Add a few LED screens, some flashing Christmas lights, balloon dolls and sound effects and you've got Shanghai's most kitsch tourist experience. The ride along the riverbed in air-conditioned glass capsules only takes a few minutes. It's transparently low-tech but oddly mind-altering nonetheless.

Overpriced at RMB50, it nevertheless beats the grinding traffic or packed subway crossing options at peak hours.

Another fun way to cross the river is via the local ferry services that thread between the barge traffic on the busy Huangpu. There are numerous lines and stops along the river but the most convenient runs between the Shiliupu dock at the south end of the Bund and Dongchang Road in Pudong. The trip is a bargain at RMB2. Have your camera ready because the views on the short 10-minute crossing are spectacular.

Bund Sightseeing Tunnel; 300 Zhongshan No. 1 Road East; tel: 5888 6000; daily 8am–10.30pm; map E6

Sample **Shanghai fine dining** at the waterfront's **gourmet hotspots**

As Shanghai's culinary reputation diversifies, and international and local chefs raise the creativity quotient, The Bund has become the city's most fashionable dining destination. **M on the Bund** (*pictured*; 7/F, 20 Guangdong Road; tel: 6350 9988; www.m-restaurantgroup.com; map E2) kick-started smart Bund dining back in 1999. Today, it retains an A-list status thanks to a large menu of seasonal and steadfast modern European favourites including slowly baked, salt-encased leg of lamb doused with Syrian spices, and the creamy M pavlova. Book well in advance for Sunday brunch on the riverfront terrace.

Culinary celebrity Jean Georges Vongerichten opened his first restaurant outside New York at **Three on the Bund** (17 Guangdong Road; tel: 6321 7733; www.threeonthebund.com; map D2) in 2004. The updated 1920s decor, seasonally focused menus and 500-label wine list quickly established a loyal following. Exquisite modern French dishes include house smoked salmon on pomme maxim with caviar and crème fraîche, and the signature chocolate molten cake.

At **Mr & Mrs Bund** (6/F, 18 Zhongshan No. 1 Road East; tel: 6323 9898; www.mmbund. com; map D5) French chef Paul Pairet steers the menu between modern European and molecular gastronomy. His inventiveness attracts a hipster/foodie crowd with dishes like duck foie gras mousse with raisin hazelnut crumble. The upbeat interiors and swish cocktail bar add extra levity.

Helmed by Michelin-starred chef Tang Chi Keung, **Yi Long Court** (The Peninsula Shanghai, 32 Zhongshan No. 1 Road East; tel: 2327 2888; www.peninsula.com/shanghai; map D7) serves dim sum and contemporary Cantonese dishes in an elegant 1930s-style dining room. The ever-evolving menu features exotic plates like shredded smoked Qing Yuan chicken with pu'er tea, and pan-fried scallops stuffed with minced shrimps in black bean sauce.

Don designer shades and **drink in the views** from the Bund's finest **rooftop terraces**

Many of the historic mansions along the Bund were built with sweeping stone balconies and rooftop terraces for their occupants to enjoy the sunshine and views of jetties and junks working the river. Today, the postcard-perfect backdrop of thrusting glass towers on the Pudong river bank offsets views of the waterway action.

On the top floor of **Three on the Bund** (17 Guangdong Road; tel: 6321 0909; www.threeonthebund. com; map D7) – which sports a slinky Michael Graves-designed interior behind its stern neoclassical facade – **New Heights'** seventh-storey terrace is one of the Bund's finest. The wraparound verandah takes in the curvature of the Bund to the north and the entire Pudong skyline. For an extra exclusive perch, book a table for two in the private stone cupola.

Opened in 2011, the **Swatch Art Peace Hotel** (23 Nanjing Road East; tel: 2329 8522; www. shookrestaurantshanghai.com; map D5) revitalised the stately Edwardian Palace Hotel at the centre of the Bund. Climb to the top of the antique staircase to drink in grandstand sixth-floor river views from the large alfresco rooftop lounge. Split-level penthouse restaurant **Shook!** serves creative cocktails and pan-Asian plates.

At the north end of the Bund, the stone edifice of the **Peninsula Shanghai** (32 Zhongshan No. 1 Road East; tel: 2327 6756; www. peninsula.com; map D7) is half-a-century younger than its grandee neighbours but has continued the timeless tradition of incorporating a fine riverfront terrace. Ascend the illuminated staircase of **Sir Elly's** through the Mediterranean restaurant and step out to breathtaking 14th-floor vistas of the Bund and Pudong from the stepped rooftop lounge.

Pick up classy **local designer souvenirs** at a clutch of unique **Bund boutiques**

Giorgio Armani pioneered luxury Bund-front shopping with his flagship boutique at Three on the Bund in 2004. Now you'll find everything from Dolce & Gabbana (No.6) and Taiwanese Shiatzy Chen (No.9), to Cartier (No.18) and Chanel at The Peninsula Arcade. Between all this bling, a clutch of local designers' boutiques tucked away in the alleys offer some of Shanghai's most delightful souvenir hunting.

At **Blue China White**, craftsmen create hand-cast and painted porcelain fired in the ancient imperial kilns of Jingdezhen. The tableware and one-off furniture pieces have a smart, modern aesthetic and often incorporate bamboo or antique woods. Next door, **Suzhou Cobblers** is the go-to spot for traditional handmade silk slippers and totes. Inspired by 1930s Shanghai, designer Denise Huang has revived this classic footwear with updated colours and hand-embroidered motifs, like mandarin ducks, plum blossoms and pom-poms. There are also retro handbags and silk lanterns.

Tucked away down Lane 8, behind a large red door, **Annabel Lee**'s sassy showroom displays a range of quality, embroidered silk pouches, cushions, shawls and leisurewear using classic Chinese leitmotifs. Next door, **Life Gallery** sells filmy-soft Mongolian cashmere clothing and accessories.

For a more contemporary look, **Younik** on the second floor of Bund 18 carries savvy fashions by local designers, including gorgeous updated versions of the classic form-fitting *qipao* by **Jane Zhu**.

Blue China White; Rm 103, 17 Fuzhou Road; map D3
Annabel Lee; No. 1, Lane 8, Zhongshan No. 1 Road East; map D3
Younik; 2/F, 18 Zhongshan No. 1 Road East; map D5

Party into the night at a private members' club, retro jazz bar or chilled **DJ lounge**

As the neon skyline ignites each evening, so does the nightlife in bars and clubs across town. **Bar Rouge** (7/F, Bund 18, tel: 6339 1199; map D5) draws the late-night crowds with a heady mix of DJ beats, flamboyant cocktails and loads of attitude. A seventh-floor terrace yields super views of the Bund and the glittering Pudong skyline.

One block back from the Bund, **M1NT** (24/F, 318 Fuzhou Road; tel: 6391 28116; www.m1ntglobal.com; map B2) bills itself as a private shareholders' club, but most nights it is possible to slink into this cavernous venue that draws visiting celebs and local party folk alike. Occupying the entire 24th floor penthouse of a modern skytower, the 360-degree views of Shanghai by night are matched by an equally dazzling interior of chain mail curtains, saucy murals and a vast tank filled with black and white reef-tip sharks. A roster of DJs keeps the dance floor heaving on Thursday, Friday and Saturday nights. For more chilled lounging, head to the cocktail bar or alfresco rooftop.

The **House of Blues and Jazz** (60 Fuzhou Road; map D3) recalls Shanghai's 1930s Jazz Age. In a beautifully restored heritage villa behind the Bund, retired TV and radio personality Lin Dongfu has revived the Art Deco ambience and syncopated soundtrack of his youth. Expect fat cigars, stiff G&Ts and a musical roster of top jazz and blues bands from the international circuit.

Hong Kong DJ Joel Lai's intimate club **Drop** (55 Yuanmingyuan Road; tel: 6329 1373; map C6) heats up after midnight as scenesters file into the gilded interiors to drape across red Chesterfield sofas, nibble on Japanese teppanyaki, and gyrate in the direction of the revered DJ podium.

Catch a chamber recital, literary conversation or cabaret act at the pioneering **Glamour Bar**

Shanghai is no stranger to elegant cocktail lounges serving glamorous drinks at high prices. But appealing to the hip set was only ever part of **Glamour Bar**'s appeal. The Bund-front pioneer has always set itself more diverse aims, and functions as an unofficial cultural centre as well as a glam nightspot.

Until June 2006, Glamour Bar was an, albeit swanky, adjunct to Australian chef Michelle Garnout's M on the Bund restaurant in the neoclassical 1920s Nissin Shipping Building. As both venues expanded, the bar moved to its own 6th-floor space and a glamorous new era began. Its stunning interior is dressed with period furnishings, a burlesque mural, art-deco lamps, and a pink-lit chrome and mirror bar, all framed by a superlative Huangpu river view.

Beyond the glamour is real substance. Since 2003, Glamour Bar has hosted the annual Shanghai International Literary Festival, the first of its kind in the city. Held each March, it has attracted writers of the calibre of Andre Brink, Thomas Keneally, Gore Vidal, Su Tong, Amy Tan, Arundhati Roy and Jan Morris. Yearlong, however, Glamour Bar's Sunday afternoon author and architectural history talks are also enjoyed by a large crowd over tea and nibbles.

Eclecticism is another Glamour byword. Its cultural offerings extend to DJ sets, big band and chamber music concerts, avant-garde burlesque cabaret, modern Chinese dance, performance art and gospel choir performances. A cultural heavyweight and glamour kitten rolled into one.

Glamour Bar; 6/F, No. 5 The Bund (entrance on Guangdong Road); tel: 6329 3751; www.m-theglamourbar.com; daily 5pm–late; map D2

Reach exalted heights of Bund indulgence with a **deluxe spa treatment**

The only **Evian Spa** outside France occupies the second floor of the Michael Graves designed Three on the Bund. A 35 metre- (115ft) high triangular atrium, oversized Japanese rock garden and rivers of Evian water create a striking passageway into this peaceful sanctum. Choose from high-tech European beauty treatments and traditional Eastern therapies (ear candling, anyone?). Or if you are planning a night on the town, make sure your nails are primed and hair is coiffed with one of the fast-fix treatments. Barbers by Three offers shaves, hair cuts and Shanghainese pedicures for men in private cubicles.

Across the road, below the Glamour Bar, the ravishing **Bund Five Spa Oasis** is adorned with lotus pools, antique furniture and spine-tingling Bund views. As well as deluxe body treatments, such as four-hand and lomi lomi massages, there are exotic half and full-day Oriental themed packages. Splash out an extra RMB380 with any treatment and they'll run you a Bund-side bath, where you can soak in a whirlpool of rose petals whilst gazing out at the stone facades and Pudong skyline through old Shanghai window panes. Lush.

The **Peninsula Spa** (*pictured*) by ESPA at the north section of the Bund evokes the glamorous appeal of The Great Gatsby movie set. Localised treatments include the Bamboo Harmoniser massage incorporating heated bamboo sticks that stimulate your *qi* and Oriental Thermal Infusion using Chinese herbal poultices to soothe muscles.

Evian Spa; 2/F, Three on the Bund, 17 Guangdong Road; tel: 6321 6622; www.threeonthebund.com; map E2
Bund Five Spa Oasis; 5-6/F, 20 Guangdong Road; tel: 6321 9135; www.bundfivespaoasis.com; map D2
Peninsula Spa by ESPA; 3/F, 32 Zhongshan No. 1 Road East; tel: 2327 6756; www.peninsula.com; map D7

Take in a **Shanghai movie** and see **the Bund of yesteryear** in one of its many starring roles

Marlene Dietrich DANS SHANGHAI EXPRESS

Ever since the first talkies were produced, Shanghai has been used as an exotic backdrop for films, and its name has featured in countless movie titles. *Shanghai Love, Exiled to Shanghai, Incident in Shanghai, Shadows over Shanghai, Shanghai Madness, Shanghai Gesture* and *Shanghai Express* were all big hits in the 1930s and '40s. Four decades later, Madonna failed to reprise the genre in *Shanghai Surprise* (1986). Zhang Yimou's *Shanghai Triad* (1995) was far more authentic, and Wang Ziaoshuai's *Shanghai Dreams* won the Prix du Jury at the 2005 Cannes film festival.

The Bund makes several appearances in Steven Spielberg's *Empire of the Sun*, an adaptation of JG Ballard's memoir of his school days in Japanese-occupied Shanghai. The opening scene was filmed at the Holy Trinity church just behind the Bund (p.42), and another memorable scene shows child actor Christian Bale staring out from the Peace Hotel. While filming *The White Countess* (2004) starring Ralph Fiennes and Natasha Richardson, Merchant Ivory brought black vintage cars, Sikh police officers and fedora hats back to several locations on the Bund. *The Painted Veil,* a period drama based on Somerset Maugham's novel, features a CGI-enhanced image of the Bund and Huangpu River. Most recently, the riverside also featured in the World War II movie, *Shanghai* starring John Cusack and Gong Li, released in 2010.

SHANGHAI CINEMAS
Despite the preponderance of cheap counterfeit DVDs, cineplexes continue to be popular in Shanghai. Most Chinese films are shown without subtitles. Hollywood blockbusters (often censored) are screened in English only at selected cinemas – see www.cityweekend.com.cn. The Royal Asiatic Society (www.royalasiatic society.org.cn) occasionally screens vintage Chinese movies.

Climb the **Bund Signal Tower** for an unusual **coffee or cocktail break**

The striking russet-and-white striped Signal Tower at the southern end of The Bund was erected in 1907 as part of a weather warning system set up by French Jesuits (the tower was originally named the Gutzlaff Tower, after a German missionary). Its 31-metre (100ft) semaphore tower served as a control and weather station for Huangpu River traffic. A lucky survivor of the 1993 widening of Zhongshan Road, the structure was carefully hauled 20 metres (65ft) to its present site, right in the middle of the pedestrian promenade.

For the price of a coffee or cocktail you can explore the interiors of this Art Nouveau landmark, now transformed into the **Atanu Café & Lounge Bar**. The ground floor walls display black and white archival pictures of the Bund. A narrow spiral staircase leads to the retro bar and rooftop terrace below the mast. With shady umbrellas, a rousing sound system and superb views, this is a unique spot to take a break on a sunny day. The menu of coffees, mixers and snacks is fairly basic, but watching barges course up and down the river, passengers pouring on and off the ferry and streams of pedestrians pose for pictures along the Bund from this sunny signal perch is a delightful pastime.

Atanu Café & Lounge Bar; 1 Zhongshan No. 2 Road; tel: 3313 0871; daily noon–2am; map E2

Explore the atmospheric **backstreets of the Bund**

The bustling streets behind the Bund are some of the most thrillingly atmospheric in the city. The avenues and lanes between Henan Road and the Bund rival the riverfront for architectural drama, but are generally in a more original (read: run-down, ungentrified) state.

Behind the Waldorf Astoria hotel, the neoclassical gem at **93 Guangdong Road** (map D2) is one of this area's finest. Dating from 1910, its original interiors are even more spectacular. Now a bank, it is possible to peek inside the Byzantine-style entrance with dramatic Doric columns, mottled marbles, dolomite roof mosaics and stained glass windows.

Continue north along Sichuan Road, watching out for the mad motorcyclists that career along this stretch. At **125 Sichuan Middle Road** (map D2) the headquarters of the Xinhua News Group occupies a grandiose, if dilapidated, 1922 neoclassical mansion. Much of the former Baroque detailing on the facade was lost during the Cultural Revolution and in its place were written slogans in large Chinese characters extolling the virtues of Mao and Maoism. Although almost all of these revolutionary reminders have been wiped off city walls, if you look carefully you can still see the outline of the Maoist characters on this old building.

Turn left onto Fuzhou Road and you'll soon come to a remarkable crossroads. Four stony heritage frontages encircle the intersection of Fuzhou Road and Jiangxi Road (map C3), including the almost identical facades of **Hamilton House** and the **Metropole Hotel**, erected by Palmer & Turner in 1933 and 1934 respectively.

At 185 Sichuan Middle Road, the **Pearl Lam Design gallery** (tel: 3307 0838; www.pearllam.com; map D3) showcases cutting-edge Chinese artworks.

Continue north on Jiangxi Road following the wall of the Renaissance-style **Shanghai Municipal Council building** (map C3) opened in 1922 and encompassing an entire city block. This was the seat of authority during the days of the British Concession. Some great archival photographs of the building hang in the marbled entrance.

Stop for dumplings and tea at the little local stalls that line the backstreets. Alternatively, head one block east to the Bund for the various decadent dining and entertainment options on the riverfront.

Go on a mini **pilgrimage** to historic **places of Christian worship**

Shanghai in the early 20th century was the archetypal Sin City. One preacher famously declared from a Shanghai pulpit that if God allowed the city to continue to exist, 'He owed an apology to Sodom and Gomorrah'. For those seeking redemption from Shanghai's wicked 1930s ways, there were over 30 churches and four synagogues around the city.

Holy Trinity Church was the first Anglican church in Shanghai. This Victorian Gothic masterpiece, known locally as the Red Church on account of its ochre brickwork, was designed by British architect Sir George Gilbert Scott and served as a cloistered haven for British parishioners from 1869. Holy Trinity recently underwent restoration to return it to its original splendour. The 1926 Gothic Revival building behind Holy Trinity on Jiujiang Road, was once the Cathedral School for British Boys attended by JG Ballard, who wrote about it in his semi-autobiographical book *Empire of the Sun*.

On the corner of Yuangmingyuan Road and Nansuzhou Road, stands the tiny **Union Church** built in 1885 on the grounds of the former British Consulate. Freshly restored as part of the Rockbund regeneration (*p.30*), it no longer serves as a church but is a popular backdrop for wedding snaps.

Holy Trinity Church; corner Jiujiang Road and Jiangxi Road; map C4

真理使爾自由

OPEN FOR WORSHIP
Designed in the 1920s by Hungarian architect Ladislaus Hudec, Moore Church on People's Square (*pictured*), was the first church in Shanghai to reopen post-Cultural Revolution (1979). Shanghai's largest Christian church open for worship is the ivy-covered Community Church on Hengshan Road, built in 1924. Both draw large congregations to their weekly services.

Tuck into a **crab banquet** at Shanghai institution, **Xin Guang**

From September to January, Shanghai goes crab crazy. Hairy crabs (*da zha xie*), so named for their bristly legs and matted brown locks on the claws, are popular across Asia and the most prized come from the deep, cold waters of Yangcheng Lake, just outside Shanghai. Weighing just 180–250 grams, hairy crabs are notoriously small and difficult to eat. The Shanghainese make it a point of pride. **Xin Guang**, rather smartly, does not.

Just off Nanjing Road East, this restaurant cuts right to the chase, teasing out the delicate crabmeat and serving it – shell- and grapple-free – as a part of a multi-course menu. The tables are cramped and the courses come fast. When the crabs are in season (Sept–Jan), you're likely to see them corralled in green mesh bags on the first floor, direct from the restaurant's proprietary Yangcheng Lake nets. In today's chandelier-studded Shanghai, the 20-year old Xin Guang's low-key approach seems almost quaint.

True connoisseurs don't eat hairy crabs for the meat, which being freshwater, lacks the sweet brininess of ocean crabs. Instead, they prize the roe, a velvety orange crustacean butter, not unlike sea urchin, that lies just beneath the shell of female crabs. With the burden of actually eating a hairy crab neatly excised, the meat begins to make sense too: firm leg meat stir-fried with asparagus, for example, or a neat pile of shelled claws dipped in the region's mild brown vinegar.

There are several other courses in Xin Guang's RMB400 menu (their cheapest), but one thing you'll have to pay extra for is *huangjiu* – a sherry-like liquor which acts as a warming countermeasure to the crab meat, considered a 'cold' food by the Chinese. Order a bottle to ensure the correct balance of hot and cold.

Xin Guang; 512 Tianjin Road; tel: 6322 3978; daily 11am–2pm, 5–9.30pm; map A2

Feel the consumer energy of **Nanjing Road East**, Shanghai's **Fifth Avenue of the 1930s**

Named after the fine city of Nanjing – one of China's former capitals and now the administrative centre of neighbouring Jiangsu province – Nanjing Road is Shanghai's main east–west thoroughfare. The eastern portion of this long road, running from People's Square (formerly the British racecourse) and intersecting at 90 degrees with the riverside Bund, was the hub of Shanghai commercialism during the early 1900s. Known as Shanghai's 'Fifth Avenue', it was lined with shophouses, restaurants, luxury hotels, private clubs, cinemas and the 'Big Four' department stores, each owned by overseas Chinese families.

Although Shanghai's luxury malls have now migrated to the west end, around Jing'an Temple, Nanjing Road East is still extremely popular with local tourists. On weekends and holidays, up to one million shoppers pack the pedestrianised promenade through the day and night. It really comes alive in the early evening when the storefronts are illuminated with neon-lit Chinese signage.

Starting at the corner of Xizang Road, the commanding Art Deco **No. 1 Department Store** opened in 1936 as the exclusive Sun Department Store and boasted the first escalator in Shanghai. At No. 635, the graceful **Wing On**, dating back to 1918, had a roof garden where guests sipped tea and watched Shaoxing opera. At No. 353 another heritage building is now home to an urban youth concept mall, **Plaza 353**, with a food court at the top.

The high point of any walk along Nanjing Road is the final part, where the road widens to meet the Bund. On a clear day, the view in front of the soaring Pudong skyline beyond the Huangpu River is a defining image of contemporary Shanghai.

Opened in 2011, the luxury **Swatch Art Peace Hotel** at the intersection provides more shopping opportunities for those without weary wallets. If you're in the market for a special watch, this is the place to come. The ornate ground floor of this gracious Edwardian building is given over to boutiques of prestigious brands Breguet, Blancpain, Omega and Swatch (all part of the Swatch Group). For stylish alfresco refreshment and stunning views, finish your expedition on the sixth-floor terrace (*p.33*).

Nanjing Road East; map B5–D5

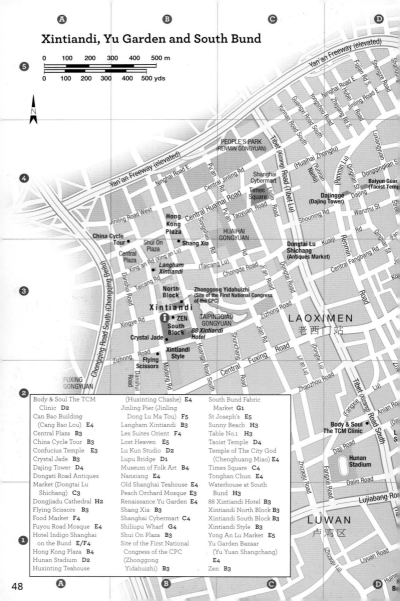

Xintiandi, Yu Garden and South Bund

Charge your chopsticks for a **dim sum** feast

Although traditionally a southern Chinese ritual, Shanghai has its own array of dim sum specialities, known as 'dian xin' in Mandarin. These are usually eaten for breakfast or at the end of a meal. Some restaurants, however, serve both Cantonese- and Shanghai-style dim sum as a quick-fire succession of small savoury and sweet plates, accompanied by a pot of tea that is endlessly refilled.

The Shanghainese don't select their plates from carts like their Hong Kong counterparts. Instead they prefer to mark off dishes on a form and have them whisked straight from the kitchen to the table as they are ready. Among local favourites are the *xiaolongbao* (steamed pork and crabmeat soup dumplings) and the heavier *shengjian* (pan-fried dough dumplings filled with pork,

and broth). Vegetables rolled in light, crispy tofu skin *(fupi juan)* and pancakes filled with sweet date or red bean paste *(dousha bing)* are other must-try dishes.

Several restaurants in the charming grey-brick alleys of Xintiandi offer daily dim sum menus in smart surroundings. **Crystal Jade** is the most popular, so book ahead or be prepared to queue at weekends as large groups of families and friends congregate over steaming baskets and pots of *longjing* tea. The extensive Cantonese dim sum menu is served until 3.30pm only.

ZEN, in a rebuilt heritage residence with soaring ceilings and lotus lamps, is a stylish affair. As the name suggests, the usual bustle and noise of the dim sum experience is replaced by a meditative calm. If you enjoy your dim sum dainty and exquisitely presented, ZEN is the place.

Crystal Jade; 12A&B, 2/F, House 6–7, South Block Xintiandi, Lane 123 Xingye Road; tel: 6385 8752; Mon–Sat 11am–10.30pm, Sun 10.30am–10.30pm, dim sum service finishes at 3.30pm; map B3
ZEN; South Block Xintiandi, Lane 123 Xingye Road; tel: 6385 6385; daily 11am–10.30pm; map B3

Visit a **political shrine** of the **Chinese Communist Party**

On 1 July 2011, China staged what it called 'a birthday party for a billion people' – a nationwide celebration of the 90th anniversary of the Chinese Communist Party. Buildings were illuminated in red, groups massed in city centres singing Communist songs, and a big-budget movie featuring a roll call of China's leading stars was released showing the official version of the CPC's founding. The modern urban centres of 21st-century China in which these celebrations were set, are a far cry from the humble surrounds of the First National Congress of the Communist Party of China – which took place in a small lane house in Shanghai on 23 July 1921. Mao Zedong and his fellow revolutionaries were forced to meet in this clandestine setting, and move around frequently to avoid the attentions of the authorities. Although that first Congress wasn't in fact completed here – the delegates fled when news of the illegal gathering reached the ears of the French Concession's gendarmes – this remains one of Chinese Communism's most sacred sites. The fact that it is now at the heart of the vibrant shopping and entertainment district of Xintiandi is an irony that would not have been lost on Mao and his band of Communist missionaries.

Inside, the museum recounts the history of the Communist Party, with grainy pictures of the original delegates, film clips showing the horrors of the capitalist treatment of workers, some fine Concession-era artefacts, and a dramatic 'Last Supper' style wax-figure tableau of Mao exhorting his seated rivals over a dinner table.

Site of the First National Congress of the Communist Party of China; 76 Xingye Road; tel: 5383 2171; daily 9am–4pm; free; map B3

Follow our trail for the top **Xintiandi shopping picks**

Whether you're looking for high fashion, souvenirs or one-off pieces by local designers, the streets around Xintiandi offer some unique shopping finds.

The grey-brick lanes of the luxury lifestyle development itself are home to designer boutiques like 'Paris of the Orient'-inspired global label **Shanghai Tang** (House 15, Xintiandi North Block, Lane 181 Taicang Road); hipster hotspot **I.T.** (1–2/F, Building 7, Lane 123 Xingye Road) and home-spun talent Wang Yi Yang's conceptual androgyny at **Zuczug** (2/F, South Block Xintiandi). Pretty presents for friends can be found at **Shanghai Trio** (Unit 4&5, North Block Xintiandi, 181 Taicang Road) and **Oshadai** (Unit 7, North Block Xintiandi, 181 Taicang Road), which both stock colourful clothing and accessories by Chinese-based French designers.

In the slick new Xintiandi Style mall, look out for luxury knitwear specialist **Uma Wang**. Her flagship store (L229, Xintiandi Style, 245 Madang Road) is draped with gothic-inspired womenswear in sensuous fabrics such as tulle, cashmere and silk, though the spotlight belongs to her exceptional knitwear with some pieces taking weeks to hand stitch.

Meanwhile, for bags with punk appeal, **Flying Scissors** (349 Zizhong Road) is an exciting addition to the Shanghai fashion scene. Founded by Taiwanese-native Tali Wu, his bags for both men and women are inspired by local rock music and include lashings of black leather, studs and zips. Find his studio workshop in an atmospheric street of tiny boutiques behind Xintiandi.

Xintiandi: map B3

Lust over **mod-Oriental designs** made with age-old techniques at the **Shang Xia** boutique

Birkin Bags may be ubiquitous on the arms of Shanghai fashionistas, but French design house Hermès has gone to even greater lengths to sate the whims of its fastest-growing market. In 2010, it unveiled a new luxury brand created for and about China.

Shang Xia – meaning 'up down' in Mandarin – presents a contemporary take on traditional Chinese design. The label's creative director is French-trained Shanghainese designer Jiang Qiong'er, whose father designed the *ding*-shaped Shanghai Museum. She works with a variety of local artisans who handcraft her mod-classic designs according to age-old techniques. In this way Shang Xia hopes to preserve and renew endangered heritage crafts and bring back the prestige of 'Made in China'.

You can find the world's first Shang Xia boutique in Hong Kong Plaza on Huaihai Road. The dreamy space designed by Japanese architect Kengo Kuma is wrapped in cloud-like layers of stiff white tulle. Within these clouds are capsule collections of rare zitan wood furniture, fine eggshell porcelain dishware and china tea sets encased in handwoven bamboo strands. Signature fashions include wide-sleeved gowns and coats made from hand-pulled Mongolian cashmere. There's also a jewellery range encompassing precious jades and auspicious charms. As you browse, assistants will conduct an in-store tea ceremony. Of course, modern Chinese luxury doesn't come cheap – prices range from RMB180–250,000.

Shang Xia; SL1-01, 1/F, South Tower, Hong Kong Plaza, 283 Huaihai Middle Road; tel: 6390 8899; www.shang-xia. com; daily 10am–10pm; map B3

Tour the Old City, from the **bustling Bazaar** to the traditional Ming-style **Yu Garden**

The original settlement of Shanghai sprang up some 2,000 years ago around the area of today's Yu Garden on the western bank of the Huangpu River. A small fishing village, it was surrounded by a 5-kilometre (3-mile) wall built in 1553 during the Ming dynasty to ward off Japanese pirates. Only a small section of the original city wall remains, at Guchengqiang Dajingge Pavilion on Dajing Road, however you can trace the exact contours of the Old City by following the loop composed of today's Renmin Road and Zhonghua Road. Within this arc you'll find an atmospheric Chinatown dominated by wing-tipped pavilions, incense-filled temples, a bustling bazaar and traditional gardens.

Unfortunately, most of the historic buildings have been rebuilt and the area appears as a Disneyfied version of old Shanghai – with KFC, Starbucks and McDonalds competing for space with teahouses and dumpling restaurants. Nevertheless, the energy is compelling, and the streets offer vibrant insights into a side of Shanghai often lost amidst the gloss of today's globalised city.

At the heart of the Old City is Chenghuang Miao, or **Temple of the City God** (249 Fangbang Middle Road; tel: 6386 5700; daily 8.30am–4.30pm; charge; map E4). Built in 1403, it is dedicated to the gods that protect the city and its people. Worshippers and tourists crowd the complex burning long incense sticks and bowing to the different deities representing career, family and health in the surrounding pavilions.

YU GARDEN BAZAAR

Exiting the rear gate of the temple takes you into the **Yu Garden Bazaar** (map E4) – a bold and brash, vehicle-free, reinvented Ming-era Chinese experience. Delve into the frenetic corridors and browse the speciality shops selling everything from silk pyjamas, chopsticks and canes, to buttons, kites, fans and scissors.

The focal point of the Bazaar is the central square where toy vendors demonstrate their wares, street performers awe the crowds, and tourists bounce along in sedan chairs. Here you'll find the **Bridge of Nine Turnings**. The zig-zag bridge is meant to ward off evil spirits, who supposedly only travel in straight lines. It leads across a carp pond to the **Huxinting Tea**

House, reputedly the inspiration of the house on the Willow Pattern plate series. Queen Elizabeth II is among many VIPs who have sipped tea in this pretty pavilion.

Opposite the teahouse, a permanent queue leads to **Nanxiang restaurant** (85 Yuyuan Road; tel: 6355 4206; daily 7am–8pm; map E4), famed for its steamed pork and crabmeat soup dumplings. The upstairs rooms serve better quality (though pricier) dumplings than the takeaway window, and the wait is shorter. A more acquired taste, but much loved by locals, is stinky tofu (*chou doufu*). Numerous counters around the square sell these deep-fried squares of fermented tofu topped with chilli sauce. *(For more on street food in the area, see p.65).*

YU GARDEN

At the north end of the bridge is **Yu Yuan** (218 Anren Road; daily 8.30am–5.30pm; charge; map E4), or Garden of Leisurely Repose. This Ming-style garden was established in 1577 as the private retreat of Sichuan Governor Pan Yunduan. Its manicured gardens, rockeries and pavilions offer an escape, of sorts (it is usually very crowded), from the madness of the Bazaar.

Visit a **traditional Chinese medicine** hall for acupuncture, cupping treatments or herbal remedies

The origins of traditional Chinese medicine (TCM) can be traced back thousands of years. It is rooted in ideas of balance and harmony, yin and yang. To correct body imbalances and maintain good health, TCM prescribes physical therapies like acupuncture, tuina massage and fire cupping, plus herbal supplements and fortifying elixirs. Even the daily diet is supplemented with seasonal foods that have specific 'heating' or 'cooling' properties.

Tonghan Chun in the Old City bazaar, is the oldest traditional Chinese medicine shop in the city, dating back to 1783. The multi-level health emporium, styled like an ancient temple, sells a huge variety of medical supplies, including some of TCM's more exotic remedies like old ginseng roots costing hundreds of thousands of yuan, deer antlers and tiger penis.

The store also has a group of affiliated TCM doctors available for consultations. Diagnoses start by assessing the pulse, face, tongue and body, and also take the patient's medical history, living habits and emotional wellbeing into consideration.

If you want a professional consultation in English, **Body & Soul – The TCM Clinic** is run by TCM-trained German doctor Doris Rathgeber. Her clinic offers TCM therapies complemented with Western medical knowledge in a comforting environment. Multi-lingual physicians specialise in acupuncture, internal medicine, physiotherapy and psychological consulting, and can concoct special herbs for jet lag sufferers too.

Tonghan Chun; 20 New Yuyuan Road; tel: 6355 0308; daily 9am-4pm; map E4
Body & Soul – The TCM Clinic; Suite 5, 14/F, Anji Plaza, 1 Jianguo Xin Road; tel: 5101 9262; www.bodyandsoul.com. cn; map D2

Rummage for **antiques and Maomentos** then take tea in the delightfully retro **Old Shanghai Teahouse**

Shanghai antiques are prized commodities, and the streets around the Old City serve as a treasure trove of genuine antiquities and repro trinkets. **Dongtai Road** (map C3) running from just behind Xintiandi to Tibet (Xizang) Road, is lined with outdoor stalls stacked with vintage finds, kitsch and reproductions, many of which are repeated from one stall to the next. Be sure to bargain hard since there is strong competition between vendors for their stash of bronze doorknockers, colourful Cultural Revolution statues and 'Shanghai Girl' posters. Behind the tourist-friendly cabins, genuine antiques can be found in the permanent stores, including gorgeous period lighting fixtures, Bakelite radios and vintage glassware.

On the corner of Fangbang Road and Henan Road, the multi-level **Cang Bao Lou Building** is known as the Ghost Market, because serious traders and collectors arrive in the ghostly hours before dawn. Although you don't need to be quite so zealous, this is definitely a morning destination – the good stuff is gone by early afternoon. Keep an eye out for antique furnishings and decorative pieces, rare books

and other pre-1949 ephemera, including opium pipes, old maps and engraved cutlery.

Continuing toward Yu Gardens, the faux-traditional shophouses along Fangbang Road carry a variety of souvenir knick-knacks and Maomorabilia with humorous gift potential.

For a break between shopping, climb the rickety wooden staircase to the delightful **Old Shanghai Teahouse**. Decorated with old gramophones, cut glass mirrors and other genuine 1930s decor, this musty-magnificent tearoom serves pots of tea and soup noodles.

Cang Bao Lou Building; 57 Fangbang Middle Road; daily 5am–5pm; map E4
Old Shanghai Teahouse; 385 Fangbang Middle Road; map E4

Get kitted out with a **custom-made wardrobe** at the **South Bund fabric market**

Sartorially speaking, it's difficult to beat the buzz of getting a suit or dress made and measured especially for you. While the benevolent charm of a professional tailor is sadly absent at South Bund, it's hard to beat this bustling market for the sheer variety of fabric and absurdly low prices.

The market is located in the south of Shanghai's Old Town where you can meander through the traditional *longtang* (lane housing) that's been largely bulldozed in other parts of the city. Spread over three floors, the market is a hive of vendors making everything from jeans to tuxedos.

Most of the cost is the fabric (labour is cheap) so expect to pay more for quality threads. You can either copy something you already own, use a computer printout or draw your own design, though it's best to stick to classic cuts – think pencil skirt or pea coat. Most items take a week to make, but you can pay extra to expedite the process.

WHERE TO GO AND WHAT TO BUY

For a buttery-soft leather jacket, **stall 195** has a good range of tan, black and even bright leathers and will make a biker jacket for around RMB800. Dashing tuxedos can be found at **stall 137**, which does the lot – suit, shirt, tie and cummerbund – for RMB900 with a 24-hour express service. Classic suits (RMB700) are made well at **stall 326**, where some English is spoken. Just down the hall, Eric Chang at **stall 310** makes excellent fitted shirts for RMB85.

For casual wear, some of the best prices at the market are at **stall 285**, which offers a wide range of cotton and linen and is best at copying shorts (RMB100) or trousers (RMB170). Meanwhile, **stall 215** stocks reams of luscious cashmere from charcoal to camel. It's difficult to get them below RMB700 for a cashmere coat – a good sign as it means it's pure. Stunning silks can be found at **stall 136**, with block colours costing RMB45 per metre and tussah silk costing RMB75. Finally, for *qipaos* (Chinese dresses) **stall 186** has a good selection of styles and a competitive price at RMB350.

South Bund Fabric Market; 399 Lujiabang Road; tel: 6377 7288; daily 9am–6pm; map G1

Share a special lunch at **Table No. 1** then relax on a sun lounger at **Sunny Beach**

At midday, everything in Shanghai stops for lunch. From hole-in-the-wall kiosks to upscale eateries, lunch is a very big deal. One of Shanghai's most in-demand lunchtime spots is **Table No. 1** by Jason Atherton on the ground floor of The Waterhouse at the South Bund boutique hotel. Jason Atherton was the first British chef to complete a stint at Ferran Adrià's el Bulli in Spain, and his time at Gordon Ramsay's Maze in London saw it gain a Michelin star. Table No. 1 in Shanghai, Atherton's first solo project, serves modern European cuisine in a spare but stylish dining room and courtyard terrace, and has cultivated its own rooftop herb garden. The focus is on light seasonal dishes prepared for sharing. The lunch menu – which changes every two weeks – comprises tasting and tapas dishes cooked and presented in a modern style, such as roasted squid with almond puree, cucumber and olives; and sweetcorn and basil velouté with braised duck.

After lunch, it's time to head to the beach. The coastline near Shanghai isn't suitable for swimming, so in 2011 the city created a man-made sandy beach beside the Huangpu River for sun worshippers. Close to The Waterhouse at South Bund, Sunny Beach has sun loungers, parasols – and views of the Pudong skyline. The artificial beach became such a popular hangout, that it was extended to double the size three months later, when a 64-sq-metre (690-sq-ft) pool was also added – and weekend pool parties were inaugurated throughout the summer months.

Waterhouse at South Bund, 1–2 Maojiayuan Road, nr Zhongshan Road South; tel: 6080 2999; www.tableno-1. com; map H3

Step aboard **a cruise boat** after dark and sail along the neon-lit **Huangpu River**

The Huangpu River is more than just Shanghai's visual centrepiece – it is the city's lifeblood. Connecting the East China Sea and the mighty Yangtze River, it facilitated the earliest fishing vessels whose owners formed Shanghai's original riverside settlement. Nineteenth-century development saw coastal junks and, later, barges, trans-continental merchant vessels and cruise liners ply the muddy waters, converting Shanghai into a city of globalised trade.

Shanghai's tidal economic artery pulses with an additional revenue source: tourism. Day and night river cruises are extremely popular with Chinese tourists. It's easy to see why, as the broad river offers a unique photographic vantage point contrasting Shanghai's east and west banks.

Several cruise operators (mostly offering a similar route and price point, and ranging in size from 80-seaters to a 1,000-person multi-deck cruiser) depart from the revamped Shiliupu wharf south of the Bund (in front of Hotel Indigo). The route heads north to view the Pudong skyline and international cruise terminal then loops south along the Bund towards the city's impressive bridges and the 2010 Shanghai World Expo site. Some cruises take you further toward the mouth of the Yangtze River.

The most photogenic river trip is after dark, when the skyline of modern towers and heritage buildings is illuminated, and the cruise boats switch on their own bright neon bulbs. Evening cruises run each night between 6.30 and 9.30pm, departing at 30-minute intervals and taking approximately 45 minutes.

Tickets (RMB100) can be bought at the terminal before boarding.

Shiliupu Wharf; Zhongshan No. 2 Road East; map G4

Trek to the top of the **Lupu Bridge** for **far-reaching views** of Shanghai

The views from the Lujiazui skyscrapers are pretty impressive, and the skyline panorama from the Bund is the most iconic in China. But if you want to see the city from an altogether different vantage point, try the Shanghai Climb. Not for the faint of heart or unsteady of foot, this urban trek takes you to the zenith of the **Lupu Bridge**.

Spanning the Huangpu River between Luwan and Pudong, the Lupu Bridge (built 2003) is the world's second-longest arch bridge, behind Chongqing's Chaotianmen (which pipped it by two metres in 2010). Its main span is 550 metres (1,804ft) and it rises 100 metres (328ft) above the river. Unique in design, it mixes cable-stay, arch and suspension technology, and is built to withstand a force-12 hurricane and earthquake measuring 7 on the Richter scale.

Climbing the bridge is less strenuous than you would think, as the 367 steps rise at a manageable angle. Once you've bought your ticket, you will be taken up to road level in a lift, and then accompanied to the top of the bridge by a member of staff with a walkie-talkie (which is oddly reassuring). You'll be rewarded with 360-degree views of Shanghai, from the 2010 World Expo site across to the ocean in the distance, and the dense forest of downtown skyscrapers.

Note that no bags are allowed on the bridge, so you'll have to leave your belongings in the ticket office. The bridge is closed to the public in wet, snowy or windy weather.

Lupu Bridge; 909 Luban Road; tel: 6266 3668; daily 10am–4pm; charge; off map D1

Spice up your life with piquant **Yunnanese food** and **exotic cocktails**

Lost Heaven is a four-storey Yunnanese restaurant that does a splendid job of putting the cuisine of this picturesque corner of China on the map. The exotic menu showcases 'Mountain Mekong' cuisine, a fusion of ingredients, spices and culinary preparations found along an ancient trading route that connected Yunnan with Burma and Thailand. The rich meat, seafood and vegetable dishes are flavoured with Thai spices, Burmese curry sauces and Yunnan's rich, meaty mountain mushrooms, which are widely used in soups *(pictured)* and hot pots.

The interior is decorated in Dai, Bai and Miao ethnic minority style, with exotic facemasks and Buddhist statuettes, while staff wear traditional dress and pictures of Yunnan adorn the walls. Pre- or after-dinner cocktails can be enjoyed on the spacious rooftop bar terrace. Lost Heaven also has a smaller branch and lounge in the former French Concession.

Lost Heaven; 17 Yan'an Road East; tel: 6330 0967; www.lostheaven.com.cn; map E5
Lost Heaven, French Concession; 38 Gaoyou Road; tel: 6433 5126; map p.92, B2
Southern Barbarian: 2/F, Ju'Roshine Life Arts Space, 169 Jinxian Road; tel: 5157 5510; www.southernbarbarian.com; map p.93, F5

SOUTHERN BARBARIAN
If Lost Heaven serves an exotic blend of style and spice, Southern Barbarian in the French Concession, specialises in more homely Yunnan cooking in a more bohemian atmosphere. Its hearty barbecued meats, fried goat cheese, fresh herbs and piquant broths can be washed down with a supreme selection of craft brews from the United States, Australia and Belgium.

Splash out on **a tailor-made party dress** by one of China's best-known fashion designers

At the age of 22, Lu established his own studio and the following year won a trifecta of fashion accolades: the Shanghai Top Ten Designer Award, Nokia Fashion Diamond Award and the China Pioneer Designer of The Year, catapulting him into sartorial stardom.

Fittingly, Lu's style is very much rooted in his love for Shanghai, especially its jazzy 1930s era. His designs incorporate obvious Chinese elements and fabrics but with a bold, contemporary and very feminine flair. Exquisite tailoring remains at the forefront of his craft.

For ladies looking for a one-of-a-kind party dress or elegant evening wear, Lu conducts personal fittings by appointment only in his studio near Xintiandi. Pieces take from a few days to several weeks depending on complexity, and the studio can arrange shipping of the finished piece if necessary. Alternatively, you can rifle through the racks of fashions in Lu's studio and have your chosen outfit specially adjusted on the spot.

Many visitors to Shanghai head straight to their favourite local tailor for a new made-to-measure wardrobe. But for something extra special, why not make like a celebrity and have your own custom couture fitting.

Home-spun talent **Lu Kun** is an edgy couturier to local TV, movie and pop stars – and even Paris Hilton. Born in 1981, Lu studied fashion design at a local academy and took up an apprenticeship in a tailor's workshop on graduation.

Lu Kun Studio; Room 520, 92 Huangjiaque Road; tel: 139 1699 6057; map D2

Queue for **street food** straight from the griddle at **Fangbang Road market**

In the run up to the 2010 World Expo, the Shanghai authorities cleared away most of its long-standing street markets and food vendors in the name of urban redevelopment. What Shanghai gained in anodyne cleanliness it lost in local colour, but luckily a handful of street markets survived the cull and live to grill another day. One of the least frequented by visitors is located within the boundaries of the Old City. Fangbang Road runs from east to west below Yu Garden, and the market begins near the junction of Sipailou Road.

Rivalling Beijing's Donghuamen food street for exotic snacks, the **Fangbang Road market** is a hive of activity after nightfall. Entering Fangbang Road from Renmin Road, you'll see a big white arch spanning the street. Keep going until you reach a second gate, this time of grey stone, and you'll start to smell the tang of spice in the air, and hear the sizzle of the grills and woks. The buildings in this part of town are low-rise and often ramshackle, and the people are some of the friendliest you'll find in Shanghai. Most vendors sell food from carts, grills and stalls lining both sides of the road, but some peddle other items on the sidewalks, including toys, clothes and cheap electronics.

When it comes to choosing what to eat, it's simple: follow your nose. If you see a stall or grill with a big crowd gathered around it, chances are its offerings will be tasty. Grilled skewers are always a good bet, as is *malatang* soup, fried rice and noodles; stronger stomachs might enjoy stinky tofu.

As well as tasty street snacks, the Fangbang Road food market provides a glimpse into local life, and is a welcome contrast to the excesses and sophistication of modern Shanghai.

Fangbang Road Food Street; Fangbang Road near Sipailou Road; map F4

JINGAN
静安区

A CHANGSHOU PARK

Changshou Road

Changhua Road

B

Xinhua Lu

C Xisuzhou Road

Guanglu Road

D

Suzhou Creek (Wusong)

Guanglu

(Xinhua Lu)

(Anyuan Lu)

Jurong

(Xisuzhou Lu)

5 CHANGSHOU ROAD

(Yikang Lu)

Shaanxi Road North

Yu Fo Si (Jade Buddha Temple)

Jiangning Road

Haifang Lu

(Huai'an Rd)

(Huai'an Lu)

Xinhui Road

Anyuan Road

Renhe Road

(Shaanxi Beilu)

Huai'an Rd

Jiaozhou Road

Changde

Yikang Road

Haifang Road

(Changping Lu)

Changping Road

4

Yanping Road

Jiaozhou Road

Shaanxi Rd N.

Kangding Road (Kangding Lu)

Changhua Road

(Wuding Lu)

CHANGPING ROAD

Kangding Lu

Jiangning Road (Changping Lu)

Xinzha Ro

3

Kangding Road

Changde

(Wuding Lu)

Xinzha Lu

Xikang Road

Wuding

Road

(Shaanxi Beilu)

Youtai Jiaotang (Ohel Rachel Synagogue)

Veg Lif

Pure Tai Chi

Majestic Theatre

(Beijing Xilu)

Apsara Spa

Nanyang Rd.

CITIC Square

2

Wuding Road

Xinzha Road

Liaozhou Road

Beijing Road West

Urbn Hotel

Downstairs with David Laris

Yuyuan Road

Tongren Rd.

Boolong Home

Lynn

Shanghai Shangcheng (Shanghai Centre)

Green Massage

Plaza 66

Element Fresh

Baker & Spice

Shaanxi Rd N.

WANHANGDU ROAD (WANHANGDU LU)

Wanhangdu Lu

Wulumuqi Lu

Yuyuan Road

Changde Lu

Nanjing

Xilu

Tongren Lu

Shanghai Zhanlan Zhongxin (Shanghai Exhibition Centre)

Weihai Rd

Paramount Club

Jingan Si (Jing An Temple)

Jiu Guang City Plaza

Anantara Spa

Anyi Road

Hengshan Male Biehu Fandian (Moller Vulla)

1

Yuyuan Road (Yuyuan Lu)

Nanjing Road West

Huashan

JINGAN TEMPLE

Shi Shaonian Gong (Marble Hall / Municipal Children's Palace)

JINGAN GONGYUAN (JING AN PARK)

The Puli Hotel and Spa

(elevated)

Yan'an Freeway

Cashbox Party World

Road

A

B

C

D

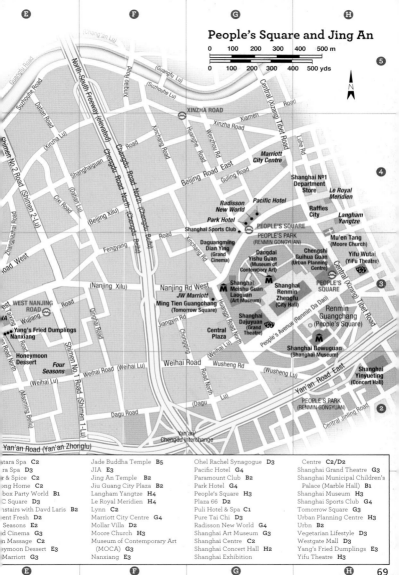

People's Square and Jing An

0 100 200 300 400 500 m

0 100 200 300 400 500 yds

E **F** **G** **H**

5

(Chang'an Lu)

Guangfu Road

(Guangfu Lu)

Suzhouhe Road

(Suzhouhe Lu)

Dadian Road

Dadian Lu

North-South Freeway (elevated)

Xinling Road

Xinchang Road

XINZHA ROAD

Xinzha Road

Xiamen

Road

Central (Xizang) Tibet Road

4

Shimen No.2 Road (Shimen 2-Lu)

Cixi Road

Cixi Lu

Shanghaiguan

Chengdu Road North (Chengdu Beilu)

Xinchang Road

Huangpi Road

Wenzhou Rd

Beijing Road East

Guling Road

Marriott
City Centre

Shanghai Nº1
Department
Store

Le Royal
Meridien

Zhangzhaihe Road

Beijing Xilu

(Beijing Xilu)

Fengyang

Radisson
New World

Pacific Hotel

Park Hotel

Raffles
City

Langham
Yangtze

3

Road West

(Nanjing Xilu)

Nanjing Rd West

Xinchang Rd

PEOPLE'S SQUARE

Shanghai Sports Club

Daguangming
Dian Ying
(Grand
Cinema)

PEOPLE'S PARK
(RENMIN GONGYUAN)

Dangdai
Yishu Guan
(Museum of
Contemporary Art)

Chengshi
Guihua Guan
(Urban Planning
Centre)

Mu'en Tang
(Moore Church)

Yifu Wutai
(Yifu Theatre)

WEST NANJING
ROAD

Wujiang

JW Marriott

Ming Tien Guangchang
(Tomorrow Square)

Qinjiao Road

Shanghai
Meishu Guan
Laoguan
(Art Museum)

Shanghai
Renmin
Zhengfu
(City Hall)

PEOPLE'S
SQUARE

Yang's Fried Dumplings
Nanxiang

Shimen No.1 Road (Shimen 1-Lu)

Huangpi Road North

Jiangyin Rd

Chongqing

Central
Plaza

Shanghai
Dajuyuan
(Grand
Theatre)

People's Avenue (Renmin Da Dao)

Renmin
Guangchang
(People's Square)

Honeymoon
Dessert

Four
Seasons

(Weihai Lu)

Weihai Road (Weihai Lu)

Wusheng Rd

Weihai Road
North

(Wusheng Lu)

Shanghai Bowuguan
(Shanghai Museum)

Maoming Beilu

Road North

Dagu Road

Dagu Road

Yan'an
Chengdu Interchange

(Dagu)

People's Avenue (Renmin Da Dao)

Central Jining Rd

PEOPLE'S PARK
(RENMIN GONGYUAN)

Shanghai
Yinyueting
(Concert Hall)

2

Yan'an Road (Yan'an Zhonglu)

atara Spa **C2**	Jade Buddha Temple **B5**	Ohel Rachel Synagogue **D3**	Centre **C2/D2**
ra Spa **D3**	JIA **E3**	Pacific Hotel **G4**	Shanghai Grand Theatre **G3**
r & Spice **C2**	Jing An Temple **B2**	Paramount Club **B2**	Shanghai Municipal Children's
ng Home **C2**	Jiu Guang City Plaza **B2**	Park Hotel **G4**	Palace (Marble Hall) **B1**
box Party World **B1**	Langham Yangtze **H4**	People's Square **H3**	Shanghai Museum **H3**
C Square **D3**	Le Royal Meridien **H4**	Plaza 66 **D2**	Shanghai Sports Club **G4**
nstairs with David Laris **B2**	Lynn **C2**	Puli Hotel & Spa **C1**	Tomorrow Square **G3**
ent Fresh **D2**	Marriott City Centre **G4**	Pure Tai Chi **D3**	Urban Planning Centre **H3**
Seasons **E2**	Mollar Villa **D2**	Radisson New World **G4**	Urbn **B2**
d Cinema **G3**	Moore Church **H3**	Shanghai Art Museum **G3**	Vegetarian Lifestyle **D3**
n Massage **C2**	Museum of Contemporary Art	Shanghai Centre **C2**	Westgate Mall **C2**
eymoon Dessert **E3**	(MOCA) **G3**	Shanghai Concert Hall **H2**	Yang's Fried Dumplings **E3**
Marriott **G3**	Nanxiang **E3**	Shanghai Exhibition	Yifu Theatre **H3**

E **F** **G** **H** 69

Go **museum-hopping** around the oval-shaped **People's Square**

China's burgeoning arts scene is often fostered in old factories and warehouses on the urban fringes. Fortunately, Shanghai's largest public space, People's Square, contains an impressive triumvirate of museums that fund and promote artistic creativity – ancient and modern – in the heart of downtown.

Founded in 2005 by Hong Kong jewellery trader Samuel Kung, the **Shanghai Museum of Contemporary Art** (MOCA) occupies a converted greenhouse in a corner of People's Park. The glassy, two-floor space is connected by a sloping walkway that overlooks the downstairs exhibitions. Although small, MOCA shows some of the more cutting-edge, thought-provoking art in the city from abstract Chinese and contemporary Indian art, to Pierre et Gilles erotic photography, Gaudi's architecture and Pixar animation.

Just across the park, the **Shanghai Art Museum** is a stately location for art and photography exhibitions. The museum is housed in the former Shanghai Race Club, dating from 1933. Look for the SRC insignia above the entrance, iron horse-head motifs on the stairway railings,

SHOWCASE SHANGHAI
The People's Square area is Shanghai's exact geographical midpoint. The main metro lines all converge here, transporting people from all over the city to its cultural and political hub. The core of People's Square today is Showcase Shanghai: world-class museums, a theatre, five-star hotels, and the imposing Shanghai City Hall in the middle of it all. The buildings, all raised in the 1990s and each one a significant architectural statement, symbolise Shanghai's arrival as a city that can compete on its own merit on the world stage.

and sepia-tinted images of 1930s race days hanging around the stairwells. Its grandiose history is complemented by beautifully lit marble and whitewashed brick gallery spaces.

A carefully balanced calendar of historic and modern art, photography and installations from across Asia and worldwide is bolstered every two years by the hosting of the Shanghai Biennale. The city's boldest and most challenging cultural festival began in 1996, and the ninth edition is scheduled to take place in Autumn 2012.

Shaped like a *ding*, an ancient Chinese cooking vessel, **Shanghai Museum** hold's China's finest collection of ancient arts and crafts. Designed by Chinese architect, Xing Tonghe (who also designed the Urban Planning Centre *p.72*), the massive five-storey granite structure opened in 1996. Allow at least a full morning for your visit, as this place is seriously large. The museum claims to have 120,000 exhibits. The 11 permanent galleries are themed on a particular aspect of Chinese culture, ranging from jade carving, coins and ceramics to calligraphy, ethnic minority arts and bronze works. A hand-held audioguide is recommended for touring each section. Two

temporary galleries host occasional painting exhibitions by Chinese and global artists. The extensive museum shop is one of the finest of its kind in China.

MOCA; Gate 7, People's Park, 231 Nanjing Road West; tel: 6327 9900; www.mocashanghai.org; daily 10am–6pm; charge; map G3
Shanghai Art Museum; 325 Nanjing Road West; tel: 6327 2829; www.sh-art museum.org.cn; daily 9am–5pm, last entrance at 4pm; free; map G3
Shanghai Museum; People's Avenue; tel: 6327 5300; www.shanghaimuseum. net; daily 9am–5pm, last entrance at 4pm; free; map H3

Scope out Shanghai's **future landscape** at the **Urban Planning Exhibition Centre**

Over the last three decades, Shanghai has been in a massive state of flux, and within this short period virtually the entire city has been relandscaped and reinvented. The Urban Planning Exhibition Centre helps to make some sense of the renovation and building frenzy that continues apace. Designed by Xing Tonghe, it occupies a whitewashed modern building with a strikingly uplifted roof – a contemporary twist on an ancient Chinese city gate. Inside the lobby is a gold-coloured installation entwining Shanghai's signature structures, which has become a popular photo-op spot.

From here, most visitors make a beeline for the third floor, with good reason. The centrepiece exhibit, viewed from an elevated walkway, is a vast scale model of Shanghai as it will look in 2020. You can peruse the entire cityscape, mentally checking off the signature buildings – including the 632-metre (2073ft) Shanghai Centre Tower, set to open in 2014.

Don't neglect the other floors, however. The first floor is dedicated to Concession-era development, and features superb old photos of the construction of French- and European-style villas and streets. There's also a scale model of the Waibaidu Bridge.

The second floor focuses on Shanghai's contemporary urban construction, in particular the range of mega projects that have sprung up since the 1990s.

The fourth floor showcases transportation developments, notably the expansion of both city airports, the metro system and the ongoing rehabilitation of Suzhou Creek.

Shanghai Urban Planning Exhibition Centre; 100 Renmin Avenue; tel: 6318 4477; www.supec.org; Tue–Sun 9.30am–5pm; charge; map H3

Enjoy a **classical concert** or **ballet** at one of Shanghai's **world-class performance venues**

People's Square is Shanghai's Culture Central. In addition to modern and classical art and the city's best museums, it houses two world-class performance venues, the Shanghai Grand Theatre and Shanghai Concert Hall.

In 2004, the stately **Shanghai Concert Hall** was awarded more than a makeover ahead of its 75th birthday. Plagued by the noise and pollution of the Yan'an Highway on its doorstep, it was decided that the concert hall should be moved. So the 5,650-tonne neoclassical building was hoisted 3.38 metres (11ft 1in) and slowly moved 66.46 metres (218ft) southeast on special rollers. The cost of shifting it out of harm's way was a cool RMB150 million.

Founded in 1930, as the Nanking Theatre, it opened with a performance of the hit musical *Broadway*. Over the years, Chinese opera star Mei Lanfang, pianist Lang Lang and cellist Yoyo Ma, among other great musicians, have all performed here. Enlarged to host 1,200 concertgoers, it is now considered one of Asia's premier classical concert venues, attracting symphony orchestras and performers from around the world.

Contrasting with the Concert Hall's classical facade, the

Shanghai Grand Theatre, designed by lauded French architect Jean-Marie Charpentier, is a futuristic glass confection with flamboyantly upturned eaves – mimicking a traditional Chinese roof – that glow magically at night when the lights come on. A varied programme ranges from West End musicals to stellar classical concerts, ballet and theatre. Among the performers to have graced the stage are Sir Simon Rattle and the Berlin Philharmonic orchestra, Japanese violin virtuoso Midori, and Ballet Preljocaj.

Shanghai Grand Theatre; 300 Renmin Avenue; tel: 6327 6740; www.shgtheatre. com; map G3
Shanghai Concert Hall; 523 Yan'an East Road; tel: 5386 6666; www. shanghaiconcerthall.org; map H2

Catch the latest blockbuster at the Art Deco **Grand Cinema**

In recent years, Chinese cinema has undergone a creative resurgence, while moviegoers have better access to Hollywood blockbusters than at any time since Mao's 1949 Revolution. Consequently, times are good for movie theatres like the revamped 1930s stalwart **Grand Cinema**, host venue of the annual Shanghai International Film Festival.

Originally named the Grand Theatre, and opened in 1933, the 2,000-seat cinema was the finest of its time in China with bold Art Deco lines and cubes across the facade, marble-panelled doors and lobbies shaped like cashew nuts. This architectural gem was extensively renovated in 2008, adding a new sound system and seating, and a rooftop bar and restaurant with views over People's Square.

An intriguing new addition is the History Walk, which tells the Grand's storied, and often controversial, history through sepia photos, newspaper ads and movie clips. Most of the narration is in Chinese, but the images are illuminating. Alongside movie posters featuring stars of Hollywood's Golden Age like Marlene Dietrich, Bette Davis,

Gary Cooper, James Cagney and Harold Lloyd, are photos of a 1954 Communist Party conference with the faces of Mao and Stalin filling two banners draped across the stage, plus 1960s posters enunciating the 'nutritional' patriotic value of Chinese cinema. These juxtapositions highlight the conflicts and challenges the Grand has faced during much of its 80-year history.

Grand Cinema; 216 Nanjing Road West (entrance to the History Walk is at No. 248); tel: 6327 1899; www.shdgm.com (Chinese only); map G3

Take an architectural tour of the city centre's
landmark hotels

Ever since the 1920s hotel architecture has influenced the way the Shanghai skyline developed. People's Square boasts a number of landmark hotel buildings worth a closer look.

When the eight-storey **Pacific Hotel** (108 Nanjing Road West; map G4) went up in 1924, it was the tallest building in Shanghai. A blend of neoclassical, baroque and Art Deco styles, its best features are the facade balconies and crowning cupola.

Completed soon after in 1926, the former Yangtze Hotel is an eight-level Art Deco monument, with bold symmetrical lines and motifs. Reopened in 2009 as the **Langham Yangtze Hotel** (740 Hangkou Road; map H4) the interior boasts a beautifully updated 1920s decor.

Next, in 1928, came the 10-storey **Shanghai Sports Club** (150 Nanjing Road West; map G3) with its mosaic brick facade and twin Art Deco towers. The front section is now the Bank of Shanghai, and a sports club and budget hotel occupy the upper levels.

When it opened in 1934, the 24-storey **Park Hotel** (170 Nanjing Road West; map G4; *pictured*) was Asia's tallest building. Clad in dark Taishan brick the

pioneering luxury Art Deco hotel once featured a rooftop nightclub overlooking the Shanghai racecourse. Sepia-tinted photos of those halcyon days hang around the second-floor history gallery.

Today, these wonders of Old Shanghai stand in the shadows of several modern high-rise structures. Soaring over the landscape is the 60-floor Tomorrow Square tower, home to the **JW Marriott Shanghai** (399 Nanjing Road West; map G3). This glassy, space-age structure twists on its own axis two-thirds of its way up, then slims into a hollow pinnacle reaching toward the sky.

Lay back and enjoy a **green tea** or **chocolate spa treatment**

The Jing An CBD typifies Shanghai's increasingly in vogue work-hard, play-hard lifestyle. But when you need to escape the crowds and noise of the metropolis, there are plenty of spas and massage venues offering unique, relaxing treatments.

Apsara Spa is a cosy, mid-priced retreat inspired by the scents, aesthetics and wellbeing rituals of Cambodia. Three hand-carved stone *apsara* goddesses greet visitors in the thatched roof entrance. This leads into five spa suites and three single rooms, plus a nail spa and dedicated waxing and reflexology areas. The extensive menu ranges from Tibetan black mud facials to Cleopatra-style milk baths. A good choice is the signature Vino-chocotherapy, a two-, three- or four-course menu which includes a red wine and cocoa body wrap and signature Royal Apsara massage with cocoa massage oil.

In the sexy Puli Resort & Spa, **Anantara**'s treatment menu, inspired by the healing power of Chinese tea, offers green tea wraps, white tea scrubs and rose tea beautification packages, plus some of the best massages in Shanghai.

On the upstairs level of the Shanghai Centre, **Green Massage** is a long-time favourite for well-priced Chinese massages in elegant surrounds. Try the rousing traditional Chinese acupressure massage or foot reflexology. Or go for something a little more left-field, like the aromatic ear candling treatment.

Anantara Spa; 3/F, 1 Changde Road; tel: 2216 6899; spa.anantara.com/ shanghai; map C2
Apsara Spa; 57 Shaanxi Road North; tel: 6258 5580; www.apsara.com.cn; map D3
Green Massage; 202 West Retail Plaza, Shanghai Centre, 1376 Nanjing Road West; tel: 6289 7776; www.green massage.com.cn; map C2

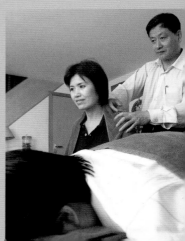

Sample a variety of plump **Shanghai dumplings** on **Wujiang Road**

During the 1920s, Wujiang Road was known as Love Lane and was lined with bordellos and ballrooms. In later decades, the east end of the road was a popular street food market of curbside griddles and ramshackle restaurants. That neighbourhood was recently demolished and the west part redeveloped as Wujiang Road Pedestrian Street, now home to the likes of Marks & Spencer, Baskin & Robbins and Starbucks.

Happily for fans of Shanghai dumplings, one of the food street's original dumpling purveyors has survived and upgraded to a small store on the second floor of Infiniti Mall. **Yang's Fried Dumplings** remains a local institution on account of one thing: *shengjian*. These doughy Shanghai dumplings are filled with tender pork and rich broth, sprinkled with sesame seeds and chopped chives, and fried in a griddle till their bottoms are toasty golden. Remember to pay first (RMB5 per four dumplings), then join the queue as you watch the buns fry in large shallow pans.

On the same floor, you can also find **Nanxiang**, another famous Shanghai dumpling restaurant with a popular branch in Yu Garden (*p.55*). Nanxiang is best known for its *xiaolongbao*. These pork and crabmeat steamed dumplings, also native to Shanghai, are shaped like little money pouches. The delicate skins barely manage to contain the juicy meat and soup, which explodes deliciously in your mouth.

Yang's Fried Dumplings; 2/F, Infiniti Mall, 269 Wujiang Road; tel: 6136 1391
Nanxiang; 2/F, Infiniti Mall, 269 Wujiang Road; tel: 6136 1428; map E3

HOW TO EAT A DUMPLING
Both varieties of soup dumpling can be a mouth-burning hazard for the uninitiated. The trick is to bite a small hole at the top to allow the steam to escape. Then carefully suck out the soup, dip in black vinegar and devour in a single bite before all that greasy goodness dribbles down your chin.

Limber up with tai chi at **Jing An Park** or light an incense stick at **Jing An Temple**

The area around **Jing An Temple** was formerly called Bubbling Well Road on account of a natural spring that once bubbled to the surface. A temple has existed on this revered site since 1216. For anyone passing Jing An Temple today, sandwiched between luxury shopping malls and a busy intersection, it's clear that the large gold-capped Buddhist temple is not an ancient construct. In fact, it is in a constant state of development as the wealthy abbot continues to add grandiose embellishments. Latest additions include a 63-metre (207ft) lotus-shaped gilded pagoda and a five-storey Precious Hall of the Great Hero made of Burmese teak.

The recently completed RMB40 million renovation project, and abundance of ostentatious gold, may seem at odds with Zen worship, but this Mi Buddhist sect has always been known for its wealthy tastes. Jing An Temple was the richest Buddhist temple in China prior to closure in 1949, when its abbot was famed for having seven mistresses and a White Russian bodyguard.

Perhaps not surprisingly, the temple is hugely popular in prosperity hungry Shanghai. Locals pack the grounds praying for luck and fortune, especially at Chinese New Year when the monks charge hundreds of yuan for entrance. For the tourist, the most impressive view is from outside, as the interiors of the temple suffered heavily during the Cultural Revolution when it was used as a plastics factory.

A much more Zen-like retreat is **Jing An Park**, opposite

the temple. This small urban park filled with shady groves, lily ponds and walk-through rockeries, is a hive of activity throughout the day. From the large crowds of elderly tai chi enthusiasts engaged in early morning shadow boxing, to the groups of men huddled over games of Chinese chess, and the couples that come to ballroom dance in the early evening – there's always plenty of activity. The Chinese garden (RMB2 entrance) has a lovely little alfresco teahouse perfect for peaceful contemplation.

Jing An Temple; 1686 Nanjing Road West; daily 7am–5pm; RMB10; map B2
Jing An Park; 1649 Nanjing Road West; daily 5am–6pm; free; map B1

Belt it like a **rock star** during a **late-night karaoke session**

Living out your rock star fantasies has become a popular pastime around the world, but nowhere has quite so many dedicated closet crooners as karaoke-crazed China. Karaoke – pronounced *ka-la-OK* – rates above bars and clubs as the most popular form of evening entertainment in a culture where alcohol-fuelled socialising is traditionally accompanied by drinking games and other diversions.

Of course, karaoke is not confined to evening hours. Business delegations frequently break out the microphones as a way of relaxing mid meeting (many hotels have fully-equipped karaoke rooms as part of their conference centres). It's a well-known fact of corporate etiquette that business travellers should have a rehearsed version of 'My Way' up their sleeves when being entertained by Chinese clients.

The most popular KTV parlours are generally grandiose affairs with scores of private rooms that operate around the clock. **Cashbox Party World** is the most popular chain, with several outlets across town. Private singing suites, accommodating up to 30 people, are equipped with a large-screen TV and high-tech audio equipment. An extensive compilation of songs is available in both Chinese and English. There's also a full drinks and snacks menu delivered by uniformed staff – it's common for groups to order several bottles of hard liquor to lubricate their vocal cords.

Rooms can be booked in one-hour or all-night blocks and prices vary depending on the time, with daytime and after midnight offering better deals. Be sure to book ahead during peak hours.

Cashbox Party World; 109 Yandang Road; tel: 6374 1111; www.cashbox.com. tw; map B1

Go for a **twirl** on the sprung dance floor of the **Paramount Theatre**

When the Paramount opened in 1934, its luminous Art Deco spire was like a beacon to Shanghai's party people. This was the most luxuriously appointed dance hall in the Far East, where celebrities, socialites and the odd gangster foxtrotted on a high-tech sprung wooden dance floor.

Today's Paramount Club is a popular weekend party venue with DJs, strobe lights and open-bar specials. The second and third floor club features low-slung lounges, LED-lit floors and flamboyant chandeliers.

Happily the classic Paramount ballroom has been preserved on the fourth level. To the left of the main entrance, the old lift to the fourth floor is like a time capsule jettisoning visitors to a different era. An 80 *kuai* ticket (afternoon price) buys you entrance to the gloriously retro ballroom, with mismatched floral wallpapers, Belle Epoque mirrors and swirling lights. A loud mix of old-time English and Chinese tunes play as the disco lights whirl and pairs of middle-aged men and women twirl across the dance floor.

You can sip tea and watch the action from the lounges surrounding the stage and/or go for a ballroom twirl yourself. If you need a partner or a bit of help with your dance moves, professional ballroom dancers are on hand, for an extra fee.

Paramount Theatre; 218 Yuyuan Road; tel: 6249 8866; daily 1–4.30pm, 4.40–8pm, 8.30pm–12.30am; map B2 Paramount Club: same address; tel: 5213 3818; daily 8pm–4am

Shop 'til you drop along **Nanjing Road West** and stop for a reviving tea or tipple

The east end of Shanghai's major east–west commercial thoroughfare was historically Shanghai's premier shopping zone (see p.44). Nowadays, the high-end brand shopping has migrated west of People's Square to Nanjing Road West, with glassy shopping malls lining the stretch between Maoming Road and Changshu Road.

Starting near Jing An temple, **Jiu Guang City Plaza** (1618 Nanjing Road West; map B2) above Jing An Temple metro station (Line 2) houses Tiffany & Co and Kate Spade, plus an excellent Japanese supermarket in the basement.

District doyen **Shanghai Centre** (1376 Nanjing Road West; map C2) is a great stop-off point for lunch, with a handful of upscale cafés and restaurants spanning everything from Taiwanese and Thai food to gourmet burgers and upmarket Italian cuisine. There's also an English-speaking pharmacy, a medical clinic and a basement supermarket stocked with imported foodstuffs.

The line of tinted-windowed, chauffeured limos outside **Plaza 66** (1266 Nanjing Road West; map D2) suggests its deep-pocketed Chinese clientele. Five marble-clad levels contain the likes of Louis Vuitton, Dior, Chanel and Cartier, where the impeccably groomed shop to the strains of live music in the atrium.

The top floor offers branches of popular local restaurants including Zen (great dim sum) and Pin Chuan (modern Sichuan). Seductive subterranean lounge Archie's beneath the Alfred Dunhill boutique is an ambient spot for a stiff drink or Cuban *puro* cigar between purchases.

Next door, **CITIC Square** (1168 Nanjing Road West; map D3) includes Bally, Max Mara and Marc Jacobs, while neighbouring **Westgate Mall** (1038 Nanjing Road; map D3) features Burberry, Ermenegildo Zegna, Coach and an Isetan department store. Between these are more moderately priced fashion outlets, such as Zara, H&M, GAP, Uniqlo and Marks & Spencer.

For something a little quainter, head into the residential lane opposite Westgate Mall. Here, the ground floor rooms of several lanehouses are starting to sprout tiny homestyle cafés and local boutiques selling crafts and Shanghainese knick-knacks.

See a quintessential **Chinese Opera** at the **Yifu Theatre**

Multi-coloured and beautifully tailored costumes, elaborate face-painting, high-pitched singing, traditional instruments, super-swift mask changes, slapstick humour and gentle social commentary are among the elements that have made Chinese opera enduringly popular. It is a highly demanding art: actors, who begin training as children, must learn to sing and dance, acquire an extensive repertoire of highly stylised gestures and perform acrobatics.

The best place to see a Chinese opera is in the round-fronted heritage building on Fuzhou Road, officially known as the Tianchan Peking Opera Centre Yifu Theatre. It first opened in 1925 as the Tianchan Theatre – at a time when Peking Opera was burgeoning as a popular form of visual and musical entertainment. Reconstructed in the early 1990s, it is now known locally as the **Yifu Theatre**.

A prestigious location for performers of Peking and other genres of traditional Chinese opera, the 928-seat Yifu Theatre (there are also nine private boxes) is home to the Shanghai Peking Opera Company, whose repertoire includes the popular *Legend of the White Snake*, *Dream of Red Mansions* and *The Bride of Jiao Zhongqing*.

The Yifu Theatre also attracts leading Chinese operatic touring troupes from Beijing and across China, plus Taiwan and Hong Kong. There are performances most evenings, plus some matinee shows. Some shows offer English surtitles on digital screens. But even if you can't follow the dialogue and lyrics, watching a Peking opera represents a quintessential – and extremely colourful – Chinese cultural experience.

Yifu Theatre; 701 Fuzhou Road; tel: 6322 5294; www.tianchan.com; map H3

Hunt out the **best cafés** for your morning caffeine fix

Tea may be China's traditional beverage, but upwardly mobile Shanghainese are fast cultivating a taste for java. Global franchise coffee chains continue to percolate across the city, with adapted menus for local tastes (green tea or red bean frappucino, anyone?). These are joined by more charming local coffee shops, many offering free Wi-fi with your brew.

For your morning java jumpstart in Jing An, follow the scent of roasting beans and hot cinnamon to **Baker & Spice** at the Shanghai Centre, a massive complex of serviced residences, restaurants and a Ritz-Carlton hotel. Run by Shanghai-based expats (who also own the popular café chain, Wagas), Baker & Spice is a tempting bakery café that brews a good strong 'long black' or 'flat white'. The large, sunlit space with communal rustic wooden benches and a wraparound balcony overlooking Nanjing Road is a great place to watch white-collar Shanghai kick-start its day. Pair your choice of brew with one of the many delicious pastries, mueslis or other treats in the glass display cases. Next door, the large mugs of coffee at **Element Fresh** are accompanied by hearty American-style breakfasts.

For something a little more chilled, **Downstairs with David Laris** serves healthy, organic breakfasts in the garden and lobby of eco hotel Urbn (*pictured*). Take a seat in the high-walled courtyard or the carbon-neutral dining room and enjoy your organic free-range eggs and chorizo or house-cured salmon pancakes, washed down with a well-made coffee – or a soy latte if you're feeling adventurous.

Baker & Spice; 1/F, 1376 Nanjing Road West; tel: 6289 8875; map C2
Element Fresh; 1/F, 1376 Nanjing Road West; tel: 6279 8682; map C2
Downstairs with David Laris; 183 Jiaozhou Road; tel: 5172 1300; map B2

Visit the **marble mansion** of a corporate titan, now an arts school for gifted children

architect got carried away while the family was overseas. The long facade features columns, French windows and wide balconies. The interiors are even more opulent, with elaborate plasterwork, ornate fireplaces, a two-storey ballroom with marble walls and floors, and sweeping dual staircases.

Marble Hall is now home to the Children's Palace, an extra-curricular school for talented local children. Wander in during afternoon or weekend class times for a closer look.

Marble Hall; 64 Yan'an Road West; tel: 6248 1850; daily 8.30am–8pm; free – not officially open to the public, so enquire via your concierge; map B1

Hemmed in by high-rises and highways in the middle of the Jing An commercial district, stately **Marble Hall** was the home of one of Shanghai's wealthiest Jewish families, the Kadoories. Sir Elly Kadoorie made his fortune in real estate and utilities, and established the Hong Kong and Shanghai Hotels group in 1866, of which The Peninsula brand is a part. Built between 1918 and 1924, the stately whitewashed mansion was made from imported Italian stone. Legend has it that Sir Elly never intended it to be quite so ostentatious, but his British

> ### MOLLER VILLA
> A little further along Yan'an Road, at the junction of Shaanxi Road, is another eye-catching historic homestead. **Moller Villa** (30 Shaanxi South Road; www.mollervilla. com; map D1) was the home of shipping magnate Eric Moller. The Disney-esque design, topped with turrets and gables, was supposedly inspired by his daughter's dream of a fairytale castle. The home is now a state-run guesthouse and you can enter to explore the pretty grounds and interiors of carved Swedish wood brought to Shanghai on Moller's ships.

Pay your respects to two exquisite Jade Buddhas and bask in the tranquillity of the temple

The beautiful ochre-yellow Jade Buddha Temple in the northern Jing An suburbs is a great place to escape the crowds and experience some Zen Buddhist tranquillity. The temple was established in 1882 to house a collection of statues that were given to a Qing Dynasty Chinese abbot during his travels in Myanmar. The monk, Hui Gen, brought two of the most impressive back to Shanghai. A temple was built to house them, on land donated by a Qing official from a devoutly Buddhist family.

The temple is filled with a number of beautifully carved statues. However, the stars of the show are the two jade Buddhas, each one carved from a single piece of jade. The larger is the seated Buddha, measuring 1.95 metres (6.5ft) and weighing in at three tonnes. The creamy white, almost luminous statue shows Buddha at the moment of enlightenment. The smaller (96cm/37in), but more exquisite reclining Jade Buddha, depicts a tranquil Buddha at the moment of death.

The jade Buddhas are displayed in a special hall at the north end of the temple. The rest of the temple includes the Hall of the Heavenly Kings which has an enormous image of the laughing Buddha, and The Grand Hall with the image of the Buddha meditating on a lotus leaf, flanked by the warrior-like gods of the 20 heavens.

The restaurant on the eastern side of the temple serves vegetarian noodles for RMB5 a dish downstairs, and more elaborate meals on the second floor. Shops in the streets around the temple sell Buddhist paraphernalia like prayer beads and portraits.

Jade Buddha Temple; 170 Anyuan Road; tel: 6266 3668; daily 8am–4.30pm; charge; map B5.

Join local monks for a Chinese **vegetarian feast**

If you spot a monk in a saffron robe scurrying past a Nanjing Road luxury brand mall, don't assume he has struck gold and is seeking a watch or designer bag. Rather than shopping, he is most likely heading for dinner at Vegetarian Lifestyle.

Meaty flavours and a predilection for exotic ingredients render much of China's cuisine off-limits for vegetarians. But this welcoming, modern Chinese vegetarian restaurant, just one block back from downtown Nanjing Road West, caters especially for meat-free mavens. It is also egg-free and MSG-free, and serves no alcohol. The varied Chinese fare – plus neat presentation and efficient service – packs in the punters for lunch and dinner.

Vegetarian Lifestyle specialises in replica meat dishes, fashioned from tofu and gluten, plus a large menu of vegetable, noodle and rice dishes. The flavours of China are well represented, ranging from veggie versions of spicy Sichuan Mapo Doufu and Shanghainese fried dumplings to Yunnan-style salted beans and Hunanese peppered chicken. The freshly squeezed fruit juices come in a range of exotic flavours, while endless hot green tea is served free to all diners.

The restaurant is paLurticularly busy on weekday lunchtimes, when office workers chow down on the excellent value RMB20 set lunch tray, featuring a selection of dishes of the day, plus rice and fruit. Unlike the picture-book main menu, the lunch specials are written only in Chinese characters – so just scan the room for someone cradling a blonde wood tray and point. The server will understand instantly.

For more recommendations and information on meat-free dining, contact the **Shanghai Vegetarians Club** at http://shanghaiveggie.webs.com.

Vegetarian Lifestyle; 258 Fenxian Road; tel: 6215 7566; daily 11am–9pm; map D3

Learn the secrets of *taijijuan* from an English-speaking master at **Pure Tai Chi**

Pass any Shanghai park in the early morning hours or late in the afternoon and you'll spot elderly Shanghainese engaged in the slow, focused practice of *taijijuan* (known in English as tai chi). One look at their calm demeanors and surprising flexibility and it's easy to understand the benefits of this traditional form of exercise.

Rooted in the Chinese belief that good health is dependent on the smooth flow of energy (*qi*) around the body, *taijijuan* can be practised on many levels, from a simple 'meditative' system of hand poses to a powerful martial art.

Although the movements themselves don't seem physically challenging, the language barrier can make it difficult to grasp the minute details of each hand position, correct body placement and focus, coordination with breathing and understanding of the guiding philosophies.

Pure Tai Chi offers daily classes with master teachers – including national champions and professors – all of whom can communicate the intricacies of their art form in English. Students can choose from a range of styles – the contrasting Chen style and easier Yang version are the most popular, but there are also specialised combative varieties like Eight Section Brocade and 24 Style (not related to Jack Bauer). Due to the nature of tai chi, classes are generally conducted on a one-on-one basis. If you've time, this is a more beneficial way to learn than as part of a group.

Many luxury hotels also offer guided morning tai chi sessions – a great way to calm your mind, and develop coordination and focus for the day ahead.

Pure Tai Chi; No. 201, Building 12, 470 Shaanxi Road North; tel: 5213 8366; http://puretaichi.yogalc.com; map D3

French Concession

B   **C**   **D**

JINGAN
GONGYUAN

Yan'an Freeway (eleva

Shi Shaonian Gong
(Municipal Children's
Palace)

Cai Yuanpei Gu
(Cai Yuanpei
former residence

Julu Ro

Central Yan'an Road (Yan'an Zhonglu)

Nanjing Road West (Nanjing Xilu)

Central Wulumuqi Road

Huashan Road

Huashan Road

Huashan Hospital

Changshu Road (Changshu L

• Xibo

Huadong
Hospital

Old
House
Inn

Huashan Lu

Zhenning Road

(Changle Lu)

(Anfu Lu)

(Wulumuqi Zhonglu)

CHANGSHU
ROAD

Changle Road

Anfu Road

(Wuyuan Lu)

Propaganda Poster
Art Centre

Caojiayan Rd

Huashan Road

DINGXIANG
HUAYUAN

Wukang Lu

Wuyuan Road

JZ Club •

Cotton
Club

Apa

Fuxing Road West (Fuxing Xilu)

Lost Heaven •

Gaoyou Road

Le Passage
Fuxing

Ginger •

• Nie Er

Wulumuqi Rd

Dongping

Yongfoo Elite •

Yongfu Rd

Hunan Road

(Hunan Lu)

Xingguo Road

Donggao Rd

SHANGHAI LIBRARY

Ferguson Lane

Boonna •

Shanghai Tushuguan
(Shanghai Library)

Sa
Taojiang

Mary Ching •

Leo Gallery •

Wukang Road

(Huaihai Zhonglu)

Lao Meiguo Xuesheng
(former Shanghai
American School)

Hengshan Rd

Su
Court

Dada •

Tai'an Road (Tai'an Lu)

Gao'an Road

@ Gallery
Suites

Guojie Jiao
(Shanghai
International
Community (

Dongbei
Four Seasons
Dumpling King

Wanping Road

Kangping Lu

HENGSHAN
ROAD

Yongjia Rd

Anting Road

Song Qingling
(Soong Ching Ling's
former residence)

Yuping Road

Hengshan Lu

(Gao'an Lu)

Jianguo Road We

Zhongguo Gongchandang
Shanghai Shi Wei Yuanhui
(Communist Party HQ)

HENGSHAN
GONGYUAN

Huashan Road

Kangping Road

Wanping Road

Guangyuan Road

Zhongguo Tielu Gongren Jinian Ta
(Chinese Railroad Workers)

Xiao Hong Lou
(La Villa Rouge)

Hengshan Road

XUJIAHUI
GONGYUAN

Wanping Lu

Zhaojiabang Road

Zhaojiabang Road

B   **C**   **D**

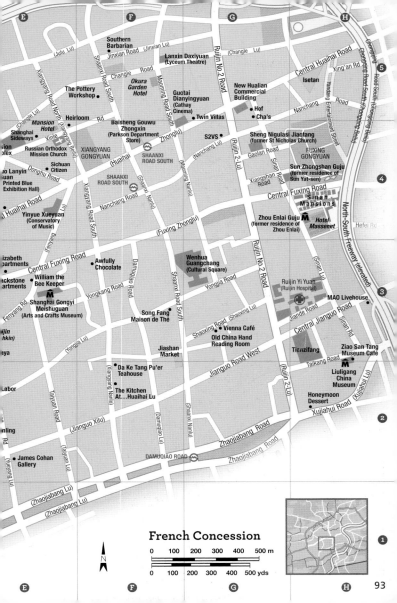

E **F** **G** **H**

Southern
Barbarian
Jinxian Road (Jinxian Lu)
(Julu Lu)
Lanxin Daxiuyuan
(Lyceum Theatre)
(Changle Lu)
Changle Road
Ruijin No.2 Road
Central Huaihai Road
Chongqing Road South (Chongqing Nanlu)
Ying'an Rd

Isetan

**The Pottery
Workshop**
Okura
Garden
Hotel
Guotai
Dianyingyuan
(Cathay
Cinema)
New Hualian
Commercial
Building
Nanchang
Road
Yandang Entertainment Street
Chongqing Road South (Chongqing Nanlu)
North-South Freeway (elevated)

Heirloom
Rd
Baisheng Gouwu
Zhongxin
(Parkson Department
Store)
Twin Villas
• Hof
• Cha's

Mansion
Hotel
Shaanxi Road North
Meiming Road South

Shanghai
Sideways
Xinle
Zhonglu
S2VS •
Sheng Nigulasi Jiaotang
(former St Nicholas Church)

Russian Orthodox
Mission Church
XIANGYANG
GONGYUAN
SHAANXI
ROAD SOUTH
Nanchang Lu
Ruijin 2 Lu
Gaolan Road
FUXING
GONGYUAN

Sichuan
Citizen
(Huaihai)
Meiming Nanlu
Sun Zhongshan Guju
(former residence of
Sun Yat-sen)

o Lanyin
uan
Printed Blue
Exhibition Hall
Donghu Road
SHAANXI
ROAD SOUTH
Xiangshan
Road
Sinan
Road
Central Fuxing Road
Sinan
Mansions

i Huaihai Road
Xiangyang Road South
Nanchang Road
(Fuxing Zhonglu)
Zhou Enlai Guju
(former residence of
Zhou Enlai)
Hotel
Massenet
Hefei Rd

Yinyue Xueyuan
(Conservatory
of Music)
Fenyang Rd

izabeth
partments
Central Fuxing Road
• Awfully
Chocolate
Damuqiao Road
Wenhua
Guangchang
(Cultural Square)
Ruijin No.2 Road

ackstone
artments
• William the
Bee Keeper
Yongkang Road
Yongjia Road
Ruijin Yi Yuan
(Ruijin Hospital)
Sinan Lu

M
Shanghai Gongyi
Meishuguan
(Arts and Crafts Museum)
Shaanxi Road South
M MAO Livehouse

ijin
hkin)
Fenyang Rd
Song Fang
Maison de Thé
Shaoxing Lu
Jiande Road
Central Jianguo Road
Sinan Rd

aya
Yongjia Lu
Jiashan
Market
Vienna Café •
Old China Hand
Reading Room
Shaoxing Road
Tianzifang
Taikang Road
Ziao San Tang
Museum Café

Labor
Taiyuan Road
• Da Ke Tang Pu'er
Teahouse
Xiangyang Nanlu
Liuligang
China
Museum

nling
Rd
• The Kitchen
At…Huaihai Lu
Damuqiao Lu
Shaanxi Nanlu
Jianguo Road West
Ruijin 2 Lu
Honeymoon
Dessert
Xujiahui Road
Kujiahui Lu

(Jianguo Xilu)

• James Cohan
Gallery
Taiyuan Road
(Taiyuan Lu)
Zhaojiabang Road
Zhaojiabang Road
Zhaojiabang Road

(Huaihai Lu)
DAMUQIAO ROAD
Zhaojiabang Road

(Zhaojiabang Lu)
(Zhaojiabang Lu)

French Concession

0   100   200   300   400   500 m

0   100   200   300   400   500 yds

N

E **F** **G** **H**

5
4
3
2
1

Meander the **elegant streets** of the French Concession, and admire **architectural gems**

Shanghai's soul resides within the charming tree-lined streets of the former French Concession. A stroll along its leafy boulevards and hidden lanes evokes a less frenetic era before China began its ascent into superpowerdom.

Start on Xinle Road at the **Russian Orthodox Mission Church**. Built in 1934 for the Russian community that had fled the revolution, the sapphire-hued onion domes sit opposite a stone-fronted 1930s mansion once owned by an opium-dealing gangster, and which is now the **Mansion Hotel** *(p.172)*. Hot foot it south along Xiangyang Road to Huaihai Road, then cross over and head down Fenyang Road until you

reach **Fuxing Road** which, with its vintage villas and canopy of lovely plane trees, is a classic French Concession street. Turn right and stroll over to admire the trio of fine Concession-era residences on the left – the French-style Clements Apartments (No. 1300), the darkly Gothic Blackstone Apartments (No. 1331) featuring two exquisite rounded stone balconies, and the Art Deco Elizabeth Apartments (No. 1327). Now double back to Fenyang Road and turn right. At No. 79 is the **Arts and Crafts Museum** *(p.109)*, a Renaissance-style gem and one of the few French villas open to the public.

Continue along Fenyang Road and through the tiny triangular park featuring a bronze bust of Pushkin donated in 1937 by Shanghai's Russian community. Up ahead is the charming **Dongping Road**, where three grand villas (Nos 7, 9 and 11) were built by the influential Soong family. On the corner with Hengshan Road (No. 11) is a striking painted mansion that belonged to T.V. Soong, the Kuomintang's finance minister. Built in 1920, this fabled abode is now **Sasha's** cosy first floor bar and elegant second floor restaurant.

French Concession walk: map E4–D3

Sip **molecular cocktails** or dine on **Peruvian piqueos** in the colonial villas of **Sinan Mansions**

The **Sinan Mansions** neighbourhood of reclaimed and rebuilt villas and townhouses, home to influential revolutionaries, writers, artists and gangsters during the 1930s, has been transformed into a dining destination *du jour*. Some of Shanghai's most pioneering chefs and restaurateurs are cooking up a storm in these stately pebbledash homesteads.

Australian-Greek chef David Laris fills an entire three-storey townhouse (Block 26F, Sinan Mansions) with four gourmet concepts: **The Funky Chicken** for fast rotisserie gourmet chooks; Mediterranean wine lounge, **The Fat Olive** (tel: 3368 9524); **Yucca** (tel: 3368 9525), a mod-Mexican micro-lounge with aqua walls and voodoo-inspired accents; and **12 Chairs** (tel: 3330 3920) an exclusive feast for a dozen diners.

Across the courtyard, Eduardo Vargas celebrates his Peruvian roots at **Chicha** (Block 33; tel: 6418 0760). His downstairs lounge pours potent Pisco Sours, while the candlelit upstairs dining parlour offers a seven- or 12-course set menu of piquant homestyle favourites.

Craft cocktail lounge **Apothecary** (Block 2, 4/F, Lane 507 Fuxing Middle Road; tel:

3368 9419), mixes meticulous old-school cocktails using homemade spirits and tinctures, along with Creole inspired fare.

Similarly named, **The Alchemist** (Block 32; tel: 6426 0660) is known for its molecular trickery in creative cocktails like the Yangtze River Tea – a sorbet-like concoction of Chinese baijiu, tequila, Captain Morgan and citrus.

Sinan Mansions is also home to Shanghai's most exclusive boutique hotel. **Hotel Massenet** (51 Sinan Road; tel: 3401 9998) comprises 15 four-bedroom mansions with large gardens and 24-hour butlers and chefs, that are rented en-bloc for a cool RMB38,000+ a night.

Sinan Mansions is on the corner of Sinan Road and Fuxing Road; map H4

Shop for **eco fashions**, **fun souvenirs** and much more in the bustling alleys of **Taikang Road**

One of Shanghai's favourite souvenir hunting grounds is known as **Tianzifang**. Its labyrinthine alleys, filled with boutiques and cafés in former *shikumen* (stone-gated) homes, offer an atmospheric alternative to the mega malls and high-end boutiques elsewhere in the city.

The neighbourhood was popularised by a group of artists and photographers who set up studios in an abandoned candy factory just off Taikang Road in the late 1990s. Other creative types joined, and soon a thriving grassroots design community was working in the alleys amidst the old residents. Now over 100 boutiques and restaurants of varying quality occupy an ever-expanding network of alleys.

Enter under the arched gate at 210 Taikang Road. One of the first studios you'll come to is that of **Deke Erh**. The Shanghainese photo-historian was a Tianzifang pioneer and his large warehouse showcases a collection of black and white prints charting the development of the city. Other boutiques can be found inside

the **International Artists Factory** (Bldg 3, Lane 210 Taikang Road), the original candy building.

On the second floor, **Nest** (www.nestshanghai.com) is an eco-design collective of Shanghai-based brands championing sustainability and style in everything from bamboo kitchenware to organic cotton baby gear. **L'atelier Mandarine** sells gorgeous silk and cashmere threads. At the back of the building, **Shanghai Harvest Studio** showcases flamboyant Tibetan silver accessories and Miao ethnic fashions handspun in the boutique by minority women in traditional dress.

In the courtyard opposite, **Kommune Café** is a favourite spot for barbecue brunches and big coffees on a sunny day. Here, you'll also find **La Vie** (www.lavie.com. cn), by local designer and Milan fashion graduate Jenny Ji. Nearby, German jeweller **Marion Carsten** (Suite 106, Lane 200 Taikang Road; www.marioncarsten.com) creates striking contemporary accessories using bold combinations of sterling silver, leather and freshwater pearls. **JIP**'s affordable range of men's accessories combines tungsten, titanium and carbon fibres (No. 51, Lane 210 Taikang Road).

Deep in the alleys, **Urban Tribe** (No. 14, Lane 248 Taikang Road; www.urbantribe.cn) is a top spot for rustic tea sets, statement jewellery and other bits and bobs sourced from the owners' travels across remote western China. **Platane** (156 Taikang Road) showcases a beautifully edited selection of contemporary lifestyle items, mostly hand-crafted in China, including ceramics, lacquer trays and hand-painted silk wallpapers.

You can't miss the huge stainless steel peony across the facade of the **Liuligang China Museum** (25 Taikang Road; www. liulichinamuseum.com). Created by film actress Loretta Yang and her director husband, the museum follows the production of the colourful Chinese crystal ornaments that have reached cult status for many collectors. Its **XiaoSanTang Museum Café** is a pleasant spot to take a break between shopping. Or sample one of the many other restaurants and cafés spilling into Tianzifang's alleys, as you watch the bustling hordes exploring this unique Shanghai enclave.

Taikang Road; map H3

Enter a world of **French charm** and **Chinois chic** at **Yongfoo Elite**

lamps and ancient calligraphy works. There's even a 1930s opium bed in the garden. The dining room serves traditional Chinese dishes, alongside other menu selections infused with pan-Asian influences. The pick of the three outhouse bars is Mission Lounge, where you can kick back on a leather sofa with a single malt and be transported back almost a century in time.

Yongfoo Elite; 200 Yongfu Road; tel: 5466 2727; www.yongfooelite.com; 11am–midnight; map C3

Yongfu Road, a quintessential French Concession street lined with photogenic villas and plane tree canopies, is far from Shanghai's madding crowd. In spite, or perhaps because of this soulful ambience, it has morphed into a sophisticated nightlife zone. The catalyst was **Yongfoo Elite**, an esoteric Chinois club/ restaurant created by a retired Chinese fashion designer in the restyled former British Consulate.

Beyond the gated driveway and tree-filled garden, the villa's dining room, terrace and lounges are an artistic tapestry of antiques, mahogany furnishings, vintage Gucci sofas, Art Deco

YONGFU ROAD NIGHTLIFE

Yongfu Road's alternative party palaces include **Rhumerie Bounty** (1/F, 47 Yongfu Road; tel: 2661 9368; www.bountybar.cn) a fun, French-owned rum bar styled like a pirate ship. Upstairs in the same building **The Apartment** (3/F, 47 Yongfu Road; tel: 6437 9478; www. theapartment-shanghai.com) is a casual-cool cocktail lounge with a spacious rooftop terrace, and **El Coctel** (2/F, 47 Yongfu Road; tel: 6433 6511; www.el-coctel.com) a tapas and cocktail bar created by Spanish chef Willy Trullas Moreno as an offshoot of his successful El Willy restaurant. Further along the street is **Kiitos** (127 Yongfu Road; tel: 6431 3787), an unpretentious Japanese cocktail lounge where precision mixology trumps design fanciness.

Take a ceremonial **tea break** at one of **Shanghai's finest teahouses**

The brewing, serving and drinking of tea remains a cherished ritual in China and every homestead has a stock of their favourite fresh leaves, be it green, oolong, black, white, pu'er or flower tea. A traditional tea ceremony involves a meticulous process of heating the implements, washing the leaves and inhaling the scent, before sipping the infusion from thimble-like cups. After watching the ceremony, sit back and ruminate on life – with a pot of tea and snacks.

The elite **Da Ke Tang Pu'er Teahouse**, set in a handsome 1930s villa, specialises in premium pu'er, a fermented compressed variety from Yunnan known as the 'Bordeaux of tea' on account of its dark ruby colour and expensive vintages. Enjoy the old Shanghai setting, free Wi-fi and snacks, but be prepared – fine tea comes at a price: in this case RMB300 is the minimum spend.

For a more contemporary interpretation, **Song Fang Maison de Thé** sells quality Chinese teas – from Fujianese oolong to Yunnanese varieties – and aromatic European blends. Leaves are packaged in *très*-chic aqua tins emblazoned with Chinese propaganda-style images that make great gifts. Sip your chosen brew in the cute upstairs tearoom.

If you only have time for a quick dip into Chinese tea culture, most streetside teashops will be happy to conduct a short tea ceremony for you to taste the different brews before you buy.

Da Ke Tang Pu'er Teahouse; Lane 388 Xiangyang Road South; map F2
Song Fang Maison de Thé; 227 Yongjia Road; map F2

Shop for the **latest fashions** and accessories by Shanghai's promising **young designers**

Shanghai is the capital of luxury shopping in China, with labels such as Louis Vuitton, Hermès and Tom Ford eagerly expanding their presence in the country. But in the last few years, emerging home-grown talent has proved chic attire and accessories can also be made in China, not just sold here.

Shanghai excels in designer brands pour homme, and one of the trendiest is young Shanghai-New York label, **S2VS** (172 Nanchang Road; map G4). Indonesian born Sean William Salim creates preppy New York-

style looks with sharp tailoring and fine attention to detail. His wallet-friendly designs are being snapped up by boutiques around the globe, but his tiny flagship boutique can be found in the front garden of a French Concession villa right here in Shanghai.

Wardrobe-sized **William the Beekeeper** (84 Fenyang Road; map E3) stocks girly, vintage-look threads. The boutique features a collection of one-off pieces by locally based designers, including house label Kaileeni and eco brand Finch, along with retro accessories and pots of organic wildflower honey from Hawaii.

Situated on the stylish Ferguson Lane promenade, **Mary Ching** (374–376 Wukang Road; map B2) is a boudoir-esque boutique, lined with purple velvet, mirrors and some of the sexiest shoes in the city. Mary Ching shoes (approx RMB2,800) come strappy and stacked, wrought from decadent materials such as water snake skin, fur and lace.

For handbag hounds, local label **Heirloom** (78 Xinle Road; map E4) creates classic totes (approx RMB2,700), purses and clutches with top-quality leather in stunning shades, and offer a name engraving service.

Go for a **gentlemanly grooming** or suit fitting in the **House of Alfred Dunhill**

Set back off the road and easy to miss is one of Huaihai Road's most handsome residences, the **Twin Villas**. These almost identical neoclassical stone mansions were built by a Chinese property mogul; the eastern one in 1921 and its conjoined twin in 1927. After a decade lying dormant, the property was adopted in 2009 by luxury brand conglomerate Richemont Group as their China headquarters. The powerbrokers' playground is envisaged as a new-generation luxury retail experience combining offices with high-end boutiques and sophisticated lounging. Luxury brand brothers Vacheron Constantin and Alfred Dunhill – both old favourites of the high-end Chinese consumer – occupy separate wings of the mansion, their flagships designed to go beyond regular retail and share the history and spirit of the brands in a mini-museum experience.

For **Alfred Dunhill** that means archival pieces and manly toys in the Travel and Discovery Room, leading up to a custom White Shirt Bar and bespoke tailoring service, plus a traditional gentleman's barber. Murano chandelier-strung **Vacheron Constantin** combines retail and bespoke watch orders with a collector's salon and display area.

The upper levels of the mansions are reserved for the exclusive KEE Club. A good concierge should be able to get you into this decadent members club styled like a European salon.

Twin Villas; 796 Huaihai Road; www. keeclub.com; map G5

People-watch at a clutch of quirky cafés

A lingering air of bohemia from its French-occupied heyday makes this trendy neighbourhood ideal for café communing. Shanghai's most charming and quirky cafés line the tree-fringed lanes – the following offering great brews, free Wi-fi and fascinating people-watching.

Boonna (1690 Huaihai Middle Road; map C2) draws a dedicated band of laptop-toting journalists and graphic designers with its strong Yunnanese coffee, laid back cushion-strewn vibe and reliable Wi-fi. A simple menu of decent sandwiches and snacks is also available, plus a little outdoor patio for sunny days. Beneath a yoga studio in Le Passage, **Ginger** (299 Fuxing Road West; map C3) serves a healthy menu of light meals, juices, iced teas, coffees and cakes. The cosy interior, adorned with chandeliers and oversized murals, steps out to a slender, sun-dappled courtyard.

Nearby, you can't miss the yellow facade of vegetarian café, **Anna Maya** (3 Taojiang Road; map E3). Inside, the small café combines the soothing appeal of a Zen retreat with the familiarity of a family cottage. Friendly Japanese owner Kazu serves light vegan and macrobiotic dishes accompanied by a becalming soundtrack of Buddhist chanting. There's a small yoga studio out the back in case you feel the need to charge your chakras.

Owned by an Austrian expat, **Vienna Café** (25 Shaoxing Road; map G3) has a chic European ambience, and coffees and cakes that are as good as those found in its namesake city.

Next door is one of Shanghai's most cultured cafés. Opened in 1996, the **Old China Hand Reading Room** (27 Shaoxing Road; map G3) is stuffed with antiques and shelves lined with literature, including several tomes recording Shanghai's heritage architecture photographed by café owner Deke Erh. As befits its vintage ambiance, there is no Wi-fi in this one.

Hop on a **bike or motorcycle sidecar** and pootle around the leafy **streets and lanes**

There's no better way to explore the flat, leafy streets and lanes of the former French Concession than by bicycle. For decades, pedal power was the traditional mode of transport in Shanghai and, with the city streets becoming increasingly choked by motor traffic, it often gets you from A to B faster than a car or bus.

China Cycle Tours rents a variety of good quality bikes – city, mountain, touring, tandem, folding and children's – along with helmets and baby seats. They'll also give you free safety advice and a street map, and can deliver bikes to your hotel for an extra fee. Alternatively, you can join one of CCT's guided tours of the city.

If negotiating the crazy Shanghai streets alone is too daunting (drivers are notoriously unpredictable), then **Shanghai**

Sideways offers tours in vintage motorcycle sidecars. The fabulous Changjiang 750cc's were formerly used by the People's Liberation Army. English-speaking drivers double as tour guides as they motor one or two passengers around the city's most picturesque routes at a leisurely 25km/hour. Groups travel in packs of between two and 30 motorcycles, making for a traffic-stopping spectacle. Helmets, Chinese army coats and rain clothes are provided. For an extra RMB200 they'll even pack a bottle of chilled champagne in the boot.

China Cycle Tours; www.chinacycle tours.com; map p.48, B4
Shanghai Sideways; tel: 138 1761 6975; www.shanghaisideways.com; map E4

Wake up to **breakfast Shanghai-style** from the city's most popular **streetside hawkers**

Celebrity chef Jean Georges Vongerichten once famously declared that Shanghai *jian bing* was 'the best breakfast in the world'. During his frequent trips to cook in his namesake restaurant in Shanghai, Jean Georges is often found chowing down on these savoury pancakes at breakfast markets across town.

Although the hygiene standards of many street food vendors may make some stomachs turn, the long lines of locals queuing up for their favourite morning snack attest to their deliciousness. Most neighbourhood fruit and vegetable markets have streetside breakfast vendors nearby, set up on tricycles or in hole-in-the-wall dwellings. All the dishes are cooked to order and designed to keep you full until lunchtime.

Popular savoury breakfast snacks include long dough crullers (*you tiao*); fried dumplings filled with pork and broth (*shengjian mantou*); silken tofu with soy sauce and condiments (*dou hua*); and freshly steamed buns stuffed with meat, vegetables or red bean paste (*baozi*). The stand-out is the *jian bing*, a kind of Chinese breakfast burrito. Cooked on a drum-shaped grill, the thin, crispy pancake is topped with a fresh egg, coriander, chives, a dash of fermented soybean sauce and a salty cruller. It is then wrapped up and eaten on the go, usually washed down with a cup of warm soy bean milk.

Breakfast sellers do a roaring trade in the ramshackle, open-fronted cafés on the corner of Xiangyang Road and Changle Road (map E5); near the inter-section of Wulumuqi Road and Fuxing Road (map D3); and in front of the wet market on the corner of Yanqing Road by Donghu Road (map E4). Be sure to rise early as these vendors and their snacks evaporate entirely by 10am.

Chill out at the coolest **live music venues**, from jazz to folk to **Chinese rock**

While the live music scene in Shanghai doesn't rival Beijing's in scope and lifespan, it's still possible to have a great night out and hear some quality music.

Jazz lovers should head straight to **JZ Club** (46 Fuxing Road West, near Yongfu Road; daily 8pm–2am; map C3) which is something of a benchmark for jazz, soul and blues in Shanghai. Located on one of the former French Concession's prettiest streets, JZ hosts live performances every night. Thanks to a two-floor layout with a gallery at the top, most tables have a view of the stage downstairs. Velvet curtains and low lighting gives a seductive, old-time vibe.

Just down the street is the smoky **Cotton Club** (1416 Huaihai Middle Road, near Fuxing Road West; Tue–Sun 7.30pm–1.30am; map D3) – the longest established jazz venue in the city. Catering to a slightly grittier crowd, its house band takes to the stage nightly, along with visiting international players.

If rock and punk are more your thing, try **MAO Livehouse** (3/F, 308 Chongqing Road South, near Jianguo Middle Road; open for performances; map H3) run by the folks behind the iconic Beijing

venue. China's ever-growing pool of rock and punk bands play regularly, with shows raising the roof most weekends.

A more low-key spot to hear decent live music is **Dada** (115 Xingfu Road, near Fahuazhen Road; 8pm–late; off map, B2) in the west of the district. Tucked away down a side street, it's a magnet for city's hipsters, indie kids and musicians, especially at weekends when live rock bands or DJs play to a packed house.

Eat your way around China from Hunan to Hong Kong at the best regional restaurants

As a city of immigrants, Shanghai's restaurants represent a veritable microcosm of China. Along with the major cuisines – Cantonese, Beijing, Sichuan – are endless variations in between.

Sichuan's seductive flavours are no stranger to the West – it's the spicy one. At **Sichuan Citizen** (30 Donghu Road; tel: 5404 1235; Mon–Fri noon–9pm, Sat–Sun noon–9.30pm; map E4), the crimson chilli oil matches the comfy chairs and paper lanterns. Among the slivers of *yuxiang* pork and the slow chilli burn, you'll find two things at Sichuan Citizen that have never set foot in a Hunan restaurant: the numbing tingle of Sichuan peppercorn and basil martinis.

The only thing numbing at **Guyi** (87 Fumin Road; tel: 6249 5628; daily 11.30am–midnight; map D5) is the wait. This wildly popular Hunan restaurant doesn't accept reservations after 6.30pm, so come early – or late. The décor is contemporary and the packed house an even mix of local and foreign, but the chefs are undoubtedly pure of Hunan heart. Order a plate of cumin-crusted spareribs and anything made with the central province's smoked bacon (a stir-fry with sour pickled beans is tops).

Despite the shared affinity for cumin, Xinjiang cuisine is a world away. The cool loft space of **Xibo** (3/F, 83 Changshu Road; tel: 5403 8330; daily noon–2.30pm, 6pm–midnight; map D4) eschews the standard 'Gold is Great' design ethos of restaurants from China's westernmost province for a more subtle approach. Cultural artefacts from Xinjiang's ethnic kaleidoscope (Uighur, Tajik, Kazakh, Hui, Kyrgyz, and the owner's own Xibo) serve as the backdrop for a cuisine centered on lamb, *nang* bread, and Silk Road spices.

The Xibo people originated in northeastern China, before an emperor recognised their archery skills and sent them to defend Xinjiang's western frontier, but

SHANGHAINESE COOKING

Shanghai's own cuisine has its roots in hearty peasant cooking, with none of the grand flavour statements and enormous variety or subtle complexities of Cantonese or Sichuan food. With its long-simmered stews and sauces, sweetened for the child in all of us, this is comfort food, not haute cuisine. An insistence on seasonality and freshness lifts it from the ordinary.

you won't find any northern-style dumplings in their cuisine these days. For that, it's off to **Dongbei Four Seasons Dumpling King** (1791 Huaihai Middle Road; tel: 6433 0349; daily 11am–3pm, 5–11pm; map B2) whose name tells most of the story: there are 16 types of dumpling on offer. Downmarket (though delicious) to some, it's not the place for a date.

If you're looking to meet someone, **Cha's** (30 Sinan Road; tel: 6093 2062; daily 11am–1.30am; map G5) could be the place. This retro Cantonese diner is so popular that small groups are often obliged to share a table. The 1950s Hong Kong set-piece feel (it's owned by a film director) is upstaged only

by the excellent takes on southern Chinese comfort food, served until 1am: soy-sauce chicken, scallops with broccoli, and the half-tea, half-coffee milk tea known as yin yang – Hong Kong in a cup.

Not forgetting the sweet, oily delights of local cuisine, **Nanling** (168 Yueyang Road; tel: 6467 7381; daily 11am–2pm; map E2) is an old-school institution serving Shanghainese and Yangzhou favourites. The decor is nothing to write home about, but the crabmeat silken tofu and 'lion's head' pork rissoles are. If you wish to try their tasty Peking duck, order it in advance when you book.

Visit the **historic residences** of Sun Yat-sen and Zhou Enlai, then relax in lovely **Fuxing Park**

During the early part of the 20th century, Sinan Road's grand estates housed a veritable who's who of the rich, powerful and revered. Socialites, politicians, intellectuals, artists and the odd gangster lived side by side, including two unlikely neighbours: former Chinese Premier Zhou Enlai and revolutionary leader Dr Sun Yat-sen.

The late Chinese Premier **Zhou Enlai's former residence** stands beneath a tangle of ivy at No. 73. The house's peaceful gardens and spartan rooms once inhabited by leading Communist party figures, are open free to the public. From the upstairs street-facing rooms you look out to a deserted villa on the opposite side of the road (No. 70). This used to be the Shanghai Maternity and Children's Hospital – and was also a KMT Intelligence Agency base that sent daily reports of the activities in the house.

A few doors away is the modest pebbledash **former residence of Dr Sun Yat-sen** *(pictured)* and his wife Soong Qingling *(see p.169)*. Sun Yat-sen was the first leader of the Nationalist Party (KMT) and was elected acting President of China in 1912. He and his powerful wife lived in the two-storey house from 1918 to 1924, and it was here that Dr Sun met with representatives of the Chinese Communist Party to discuss co-operative activities between the parties. The museum depicts the house as Madame Soong decorated it, complete with original furniture, books, glasses and manuscripts.

Dr Sun's house overlooks **Fuxing Park**, called French Park when it opened on Bastille Day in 1909. It's a delightful spot to retreat to after your Sinan Road explorations.

Former residence of Zhou Enlai;
73 Sinan Road; 9am-4pm; free; map H4
Former residence of Dr Sun Yat-sen;
7 Xiangshan Road; daily 9am-4pm;
charge; map H4
Fuxing Park; 2 Gaolan Road; map H4

Delight in the elegant interiors of a **French mansion** and watch **folk artists** at work

The **Shanghai Museum of Arts and Crafts** is dedicated to traditional local folk arts and their preservation for future generations. The delightful museum is housed in a beautiful whitewashed French villa (1905). Designed by prolific Hungarian architect Ladislaus Hudec for a powerful French official, it was later home to Shanghai's first mayor, Chen Yi.

Established here in 1960, the three-storey museum exhibits folk arts from the last several decades and also acts as a research institute, workshop and training centre for aspiring artists. The villa is divided into different rooms for different disciplines, including jade, ivory and wood carving on the second floor, embroidery, and costume-making on the third floor, and paper-cutting, lantern-making and ink brush painting on the ground floor. The prized creations exhibited in glass cases are interesting enough, but the main appeal is the ability to roam freely around the artist studios, just off the main exhibition halls, and watch creators of all ages at work. They are generally happy to answer questions or demonstrate techniques for the occasional visitor who wanders through.

The house itself is also a huge draw. Well-preserved interiors allow a rare view of original period detailing in the parquet floors, marble fireplaces, elaborate ceiling moldings and spiraling marble staircase. You can purchase the artists' works from the stores on the ground floor.

Shanghai Museum of Arts and Crafts; 79 Fenyang Road; tel: 6431 4074; daily 9am–4.30pm; map E3

Indulge your **sweet tooth** at Shanghai's most **decadent dessert emporiums**

Chocolate lovers are in for a real treat in Shanghai. Leading the charge is Malaysian pastry chef Brian Tan, whose light-textured but rich desserts, truffles and cocktails are available at **Hof** (Sinan Road; map G5) just off Huaihai Road. The heart-pumping menu selection includes chocolate mousse cake flecked with butter-crunch, creamy gelatos and Valrhona hot chocolates. By evening, the carob-toned café morphs into a boutique dessert, wine and cocktail lounge. Their signature cocktails are worth the trip alone. The Cacao Cocktail is potent but not overly-sweet, served

with lime to balance the intense cacao, while the Shanghai Mei Mei mixes vodka, waxberry juice, lime rose and syrup. Tan's exquisite bitter chocolate truffles spiked with Chinese ingredients, like goji berry, green tea and osmanthus also make great gourmet souvenirs.

Whisk (1250 Huaihai Middle Road; map E4) calls itself an Italian bistro and offers a full dinner menu, but the real reason people pack this low-key café is its slabs of rich chocolate nut brownie, straw-busting white chocolate thickshakes and other decadent desserts. Singaporean chain **Awfully Chocolate** (174 Xiangyang Road South; map F3) also deserves a mention for its heavy balls of dark chocolate ice cream and whole chocolate cakes.

For tempting Asian style desserts, head to Hong Kong's **Honeymoon Dessert** (www.honeymoon-dessert.com) which has several branches throughout Shanghai. Made from nutritious ingredients like red and green beans, sesame, nuts, Thai black rice, sago and tofu, these sweet soups and puddings taste better than they sound – especially the signature Mango Pomelo and Sago Sweet Soup.

Become a **wok wizard** and learn some favourite local dishes at a **Chinese cooking school**

Can't imagine how you'll survive without Shanghai dumplings or hand-pulled noodles once you leave China? Happily, you don't have to. **The Kitchen At...Huaihai Lu** teaches you the techniques behind preparing your favourite Chinese dishes with hands-on classes in different cuisines.

Founded by a professional hotel chef and an event marketing guru in 2007, the school is located in a 19th-century French Concession home that has been fitted out with a large, well-equipped kitchen for group cooking and a cosy dining space for sampling the results of your efforts. There's even a small garden planted with fresh herbs.

Ninety-minute classes led by professional chefs from five-star hotel kitchens are held throughout the week covering a range of cuisines and styles. All skill levels are welcome and the multilingual chefs switch between Chinese and English depending on the class. It's very hands-on – so be prepared to roll up your sleeves and start chopping and stirring.

Each class generally covers two or three recipes that you can re-create at home. As well as mastering specialised cooking techniques, you'll get to explore China's best-known cuisines,

from refined Cantonese, to spice-laden Sichuan and the sweeter Shanghainese flavours as you prepare dishes like hot and sour soup, bitter melon braised with pork sparerib in a claypot, and soft tofu with hairy crab meat. There's also a special Shanghai Dumpling and Dim Sum making course.

If you wish to expand your repertoire, The Kitchen At...Huaihai Lu also conducts cooking classes in a wide range of global cuisines, including Italian, Spanish, French, Mexican, Japanese and Thai. Check their website for the latest schedules.

The Kitchen At...Huaihai Lu; Building 20, 3/F, 383 Xiangyang Road South; tel: 6433 2700; www.thekitchenat.com; map F2

Explore the **eco-dining and shopping** enclave of **Jiashan Market**

One of the joys of exploring Shanghai's old residential lanes, or *longtang*, is the myriad surprises and contrasts they contain. Deep inside one lane off Shaanxi Road, past a lively local street market of vendors selling seafood and vegetables, is one such surprise: a friendly eco-community known as **Jiashan Market**.

The enclave is the brainchild of James Brearley, founder of Shanghai-based urban design firm BAU. Disillusioned with the 'churning out' of modern Chinese neighbourhoods with an emphasis on fast-paced change rather than thoughtful planning and sustainability, he envisaged Jiashan Market as an Environmentally Sustainable Design (ESD) to showcase the benefits of an urban garden community and prove that green living is possible in one of the world's densest cityscapes.

Originally the Shanghai Knitting Factory compound, the reclaimed and renovated warehouses have been transformed into loft residences, offices, restaurants, boutiques and a kids' club, surrounding an open-air courtyard and barbecue pavilion. Residents and visitors can grab an organic snack or

Yunnan coffee at trendy café **Melange Oasis**, enjoy homestyle Korean favourites at **Annion Kitchen**, or sample mod-Malay flavours in a designer dining room and lounge at **Café Sambal**. They can also pick up cool, customised furnishings at **Barrn**, and Zen-out in the **Venus Spring Japanese Spa**. Fresh fruits, vegetables, herbs and other ingredients come courtesy of the mini organic farms on the buildings' rooftops – which also help insulate the building, reduce energy consumption and shrink the carbon footprint of this neat little enclave.

Jiashan Market; No. 37, Lane 550 Shaanxi Road South; http://jiashan market.com; map F3

Visit some of the French Concession's most progressive **contemporary art galleries**

Though People's Square is home to Shanghai's prominent galleries such as the Museum of Contemporary Art, the lanes of the former French Concession contain some of the most cutting edge art spaces in the city. International ownership means these smaller galleries have links with the European and American art spheres, so they draw acclaimed names from both the East and West.

Hidden down a quiet lane, the **James Cohan Gallery** is in a crumbling European-style villa surrounded by a quaint garden of lush greenery and shaded benches. Spread over three rooms, the exhibition space is full of light with whitewashed walls and antique floorboards – perfect for showing the works of artists such as Alex Katz and Louise Bourgeois, who have had shows here.

Five minutes walk from James Cohan in the swanky Surpass Court (home to trendy bars, upscale restaurants and shops) **Art Labor** is one of the more progressive galleries in Shanghai. The space's exposed concrete, spot-lighting and ceiling pipes provide an industrial chic backdrop for shows from both international and local artists.

One of the smallest exhibition spaces in the city, **Leo Gallery** is also one of the most charming. In trendy Ferguson Lane, the two-floor gallery is in a converted villa with a sun-dappled rooftop terrace for pit-stops. Past exhibitions have included the bright oil paintings of Basmat Levin and sculptures from Kevin Fung.

Art Labor; Building 4, 570 Yongjia Road; tel: 3460 5331; www.artlaborgallery. com; Tue–Sun 11am–7pm; free; map E2
James Cohan Gallery; Building 1, Lane 170 Yueyang Road; tel: 5466 0825; www. jamescohan.com; Tue–Sun 11am–6pm; free; map E2
Leo Gallery; Ferguson Lane, 374–376 Wukang Road; tel: 5464 8785; www.leo gallery.com.cn; Tue–Sun 11am–7pm; free; map B2

Discover **Communist era art** at the **Propaganda Poster Art Centre**

Shanghai's future-focused energies overshadow contemplation of its more recent history. This hidden museum in a basement apartment is a treasure trove of retro China from the 1950s, '60s and '70s. The museum was created by Shanghai local Yang Pei Ming to preserve and showcase Mao-era propaganda artworks. Over the years, he amassed a collection of more than 5,000 posters, book covers, newspaper ads and artefacts exhorting China to achieve monumental national feats fuelled by the glory of Mao's ideological vision. The poster images depict peasants, workers, schoolchildren and 'model Communists' pulling together for the greater good of the motherland, with phrases such as 'Don't be selfish, help other people' and the ubiquitous 'The East is Red'. Mao himself is deified in several ways, often with beams of sunlight radiating through his body, or in heroic poses speaking to the Chinese people.

The style and detail of the Communist Party posters change significantly from the 1949 Communist Revolution to Mao's death in 1976, although the dominating themes remained Communism's superiority, the wolfish aggression of Western capitalism and the benefits of universal brotherhood in China.

This skillfully curated exhibition is a unique chronology of these changes during an era of colourful, yet crudely socially manipulative, mass propaganda. Some of the posters, plus a collection of memorabilia, are available for purchase in the museum shop.

Propaganda Poster Art Centre; Room B-0C, 868 Huashan Road; tel: 6211 1845; www.shanghaipropagandaart.com; daily 10am–5pm; map B4

MAOMENTOES
More Mao memorabilia can be found at Madame Mao's Dowry (207 Fumin Road; tel: 5403 3551), a fun boutique selling original revolution era posters, photographs, woodblock prints and paintings, along with their own hand-painted accessories with updated slogans, like 'Defend Our Stock Exchange'.

Craft and glaze your own **Chinese porcelain** at the **Pottery Workshop**

For a deeper insight into traditional Chinese ceramic-making, get your hands dirty at the **Pottery Workshop**. This ceramics studio started in a Hong Kong basement over 25 years ago has expanded to four Chinese cities – including Jingdezhen, the ancient porcelain capital of China where the imperial kilns were located. The Pottery Workshop's in-house and guest ceramicists create funky handmade bowls, tea sets, sculptures and more that are for sale in its two Shanghai boutiques. Beyond this, they also have an education centre offering a variety of classes in both pottery and sculpture, and even professional artist residencies in Jingdezhen. From the basics of hand building and using the pottery wheel to more challenging sessions in aesthetic development, hand painting and techniques such as mold-making, the experienced teachers conduct classes in English and Mandarin for up to 20 students at a time. Classes are available for all ages, with the creative junior classes (5–14 years) a real hit, allowing kids to craft their own figurines, masks, rockets and animals.

Be sure to wear clothes that you can get dirty or bring your own apron. Classes include materials, basic tools and a firing fee.

The Pottery Workshop; No. 1A Lane Shaanxi Road South; tel: 6445 0902; www.potteryworkshop.org; map F5

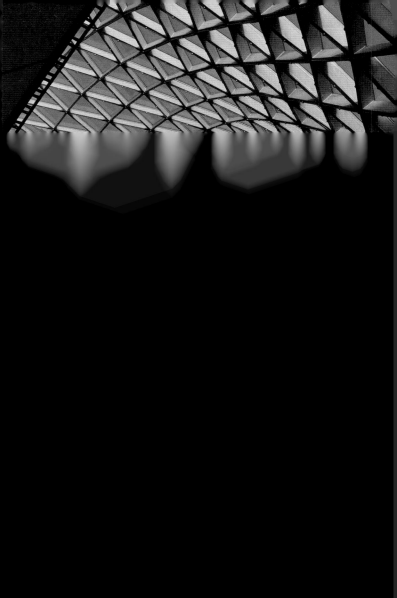

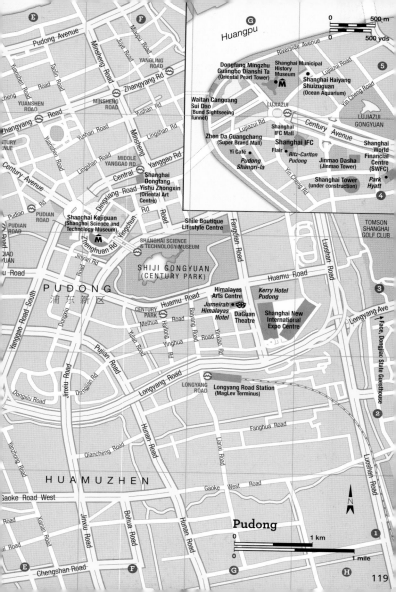

Pudong

Inset (top, Lujiazui area):

Huangpu

Riverside Avenue

Dongfang Mingzhu Guangbo Dianshi Ta (Oriental Pearl Tower)

Shanghai Municipal History Museum

Shanghai Haiyang Shuizuguan (Ocean Aquarium)

Waitan Canguang Sui Dao (Bund Sightseeing Tunnel)

Zhen Da Guangchang (Super Brand Mall)

LUJIAZUI

LUJIAZUI GONGYUAN

Yi Café

Flair

Shanghai IFC Mall

Shanghai IFC

Ritz-Carlton Pudong

Jinmao Dasha (Jinmao Tower)

Shanghai World Financial Centre (SWFC)

Park Hyatt

Pudong Shangri-la

Shanghai Tower (under construction)

Lujiazui Rd

Century Avenue

Yin Cheng Rd

Main map labels:

Pudong Avenue

YANGLING ROAD

Zhangyang Rd

Yuanshen Road

Minsheng Road

MINSHENG ROAD

Yushan Rd

Lingshan Rd

Yanggao Rd

MIDDLE YANGGAO RD

Central

Dingxiang Road

Yingchun Rd

Shanghai Dongfang Yishu Zhongxin (Oriental Art Centre)

Shanghai Kejiguan (Shanghai Science and Technology Museum)

Shile Boutique Lifestyle Centre

SHANGHAI SCIENCE & TECHNOLOGY MUSEUM

Fangdian Road

TOMSON SHANGHAI GOLF CLUB

PUDONG 浦东新区

SHIJI GONGYUAN (CENTURY PARK)

Huamu Road

Kerry Hotel Pudong

Luoshan Road

Himalayas Arts Centre

Jumeirah Himalayas Hotel

DaGuan Theatre

Shanghai New International Expo Centre

CENTURY PARK

Meihua Road

Haitong Road

Baiyang Road

Yingbua

Yinlan Road

Yinhua

Longyang Ave

Face, Dongjiao State Guesthouse

Jinxiu Road

Pujian Road

Dongjian Rd

Yuan Road

Longyang Road

LONGYANG ROAD

Longyang Road Station (MagLev Terminus)

Human Road

Lianxi Road

HUAMUZHEN

Dongxiu Road

Yanzhong Road

Qiancheng Road

Fanghua Road

Gaoke West Road

Gaoke Road West

Jinxiu Road

Beihua Road

Human Road

Xizan Road

Chengshan Road

Pudian Road

PUDIAN ROAD

Zhenghuan Rd

Jinyan Rd

Yangaao Road South

Dongjing

Pudian Rd

CENTURY AVENUE

Zhangyang Road

Tailin Road

Minsheng Road

Zhangyang Rd

Miaopu Road

Juye Road

Huangpu

Century Avenue

Scale bars:

0 — 500 m

0 — 500 yds

0 — 1 km

0 — 1 mile

N

Scale the heights of **Shanghai's skytowers** and take in **heartstopping views**

In the early 1990s, during a business trip to Shanghai, Japanese developer Minoru Mori learned of plans to build a triptych of monumental skyscrapers on a triangle of land in Pudong. These three towers would symbolise the status of the district as a rising global financial centre. Immediately, Mori told government officials: 'I want to build one of those towers'.

Almost two decades later, two of the three towers – the 88-level Jinmao Tower, opened in 1999, and the 101-floor Shanghai World Financial Centre, opened in 2008 – stand tall and proud. Dominating those super-tall siblings, however, will be the 121-floor Shanghai Tower, slated to open in 2014.

SHANGHAI SUPERTOWERS

Echoing elements of Shanghai's 1930s Art Deco heritage, the the glistening tiered pinnacle of **Jinmao Tower**, designed by Skidmore, Owings and Merrill, quickly became a cherished Shanghai landmark. China's tallest building until the opening

of the Shanghai World Financial Centre, the tower made headlines in June 2007, when French urban climber Alain Robert, sporting a Spiderman costume, scaled the exterior and was promptly arrested by police.

The Jinmao Tower comprises office floors, convention facilities, the J-Life retail complex and the Grand Hyatt hotel from the 53rd to the 87th floors. Rising 340 metres (1,115ft) above Pudong, the 88th-floor Observatory attracts more than one million visitors per year and affords magnificent vistas. One floor below, Shanghai's original sky lounge, the Grand Hyatt's Cloud 9 bar, yields similar 360-degree views – but with the added benefit of cosy armchairs and classy cocktails.

Nicknamed the 'bottle opener' because of its rectangular opening at the top, the Mori-built **Shanghai World Financial Centre** (SWFC) was designed by Kohn Pedersen Fox. Occupying this extraordinary structure are retail and dining on the basement and ground levels, multiple office floors and the Park Hyatt Shanghai (p.176) between the 79th and 93rd floors. Most exciting of all is the vertigo-inducing SWFC Observatory, featuring three above-the-clouds observation platforms. The Sky Arena, used mainly for banquets and private events, is perched on the 94th floor (423 metres/1,388 ft above ground). Three levels higher is Sky Walk 97 – a thrilling walkway with floor-to-ceiling glass panelling and a retractable roof. The crowning glory is the 100th-floor Sky Walk 100 – a 55 metre (180ft) -long glass corridor overhanging the trapezoidal gap at the building's summit. Transparent inset floor panels enable visitors, quite literally, to look almost half a kilometre (1/3 mile) down to the city below.

From the Observatory, it's easy to see the shape of the future. Rising fast, almost within touching distance, is the **Shanghai Tower**. Designed by US-based architectural firm Gensler, the tower broke ground in November 2008 and will stand 632 metres (2,073ft) tall when completed – making it the second-tallest building on earth.

Shanghai World Financial Centre; Dongtai Road; tel: 4001 100 555; www.swfc-observatory.com; daily 8am–11pm, last entry 10pm; charge; map H4
Jinmao Tower; 88 Century Avenue; tel: 5047 6688; www.jinmao88.com; daily 8.30am–10pm; map H4

Sip a **sunset cocktail** on the cloud-view terrace of **Flair**

When the elevator doors open after the ear-popping ride to the 58th floor of the Shanghai IFC Tower, it's not unusual to find a TV crew waiting to descend. Seemingly floating on a cloud above Shanghai, **Flair** has become the go-to destination for broadcast interviews using the cityscape as a backdrop. The vistas really are jaw-dropping. Elevated high above the Pudong riverbank, the cherry spheres of the Oriental Pearl Tower appear almost touchable, and on a clear evening the neon lights stretch to the horizon. Consequently, memories – and not just TV shows – are recorded here daily. Flair is Shanghai's hottest 'see-and-be-photographed' destination. But don't expect to ascend, snap and descend – seats on the terrace are in demand, so be sure to reserve a table in advance. The optimum time to take your seat is just before sunset, so that you have a drink in hand, and a plate of nibbles to munch on, when the burning orange sun sinks behind the Bund.

Flair is more than just a high-rise lounge – it serves very good pan-Asian tapas, inside the restaurant and on the split-level outdoor terrace. There's no finer way to usher in Shanghai nightfall than with a Flair Experience cocktail (Jameson Whiskey, Absolut Pears Vodka, mango puree, peach syrup and ginger) and a table spread of pan-seared fois gras with miso rice, pomelo salad with kaffir lime dressing, and drunken Manila crab with ginger and spring onion. Just remember to pack your mini camera in your purse or pocket.

Flair; 58/F, The Ritz-Carlton Pudong, IFC Tower, 8 Century Avenue; tel: 2020 1888; www.ritzcarlton.com; map G4

Fly through thin air at **dizzying speed** aboard the levitating **MagLev train**

Since 2010, China's nationwide rollout of its high-speed, inter-city train network has grabbed global headlines, but back in 2004 Shanghai sat at the forefront of the nation's rail upgrade ambitions. The opening of the magnetic levitation (MagLev) line earned Shanghai boasting rights for having the world's fastest passenger train.

Admittedly, the MagLev serves a limited purpose, running only on a 30km (19-mile) route between Shanghai Pudong International Airport and Longyang Road station (map G2) in Pudong, which is a transit point for Metro Line 2. But this is a truly thrilling ride. The 8-minute journey averages 240km/h (149mph), and reaches a top speed – at which point legions of digital cameras are hoisted towards the in-carriage speedometer – of 431km/h (267mph). It is like being strapped to a bullet.

The world's first commercial MagLev line uses 'contactless technology' devised by Germany's Transrapid company. The train is elevated by powerful magnets about 10mm above the purpose-built track, called a guideway, as it

'guides' rather than 'directs' the train's movement. Other magnets provide propulsion and braking. MagLev trains attain higher speeds and require less maintenance than conventional high-speed trains because no friction exists. Plans are afoot to extend the MagLev line to connect Shanghai's two airports, Pudong and Hongqiao. The 55km (34-mile) journey would take around 15 minutes. The MagLev is not considered economically viable for inter-city travel because the initial development costs are prohibitively high – Transrapid's technology was specifically created for short journeys.

Trains run daily every 15–20 minutes, 6.45am–9.40pm; for ticket and fare information go to www.smtdc.com/en

Bask in the pleasure of a *qigong* **spa therapy** at a luxury wellbeing centre

Way out in the suburbs of Pudong, Shile Boutique Lifestyle Centre is set in Zen-infused designer surrounds created by Japanese architect Arata Isozaki. The term '*shi le*' was coined by intellectuals during the Song Dynasty over 1,000 years ago and refers to the cultivation of the 10 pleasures in life. Updated 'pleasures' in this condominium clubhouse include art appreciation, health-conscious gourmet Chinese cuisine, a library and a unique day spa.

A deeply Chinese understanding of wellness – in everything from meridian and *qigong* techniques used, to the cleansing white fungus and jujube dessert offered after the treatment – is complemented with Western aromatherapy and Dermalogica products. Try a traditional Chinese meridian treatment (choose from immune energising, pain relief and sleep well options).

A Taiwanese *qigong* master conducts monthly training sessions with the staff and each therapist undertakes a maximum of three treatments a day to ensure their healing *qi* is not diminished. Minimal English is spoken so just relax and bask in the pleasure of it all.

Shile Boutique Lifestyle Centre; No. 1, Lane 599 Fangdian Road; tel: 5033 9113; www.jjtshile.com; map G4

THERAPEUTIC RETREATS

A spa treatment or massage is the perfect way to escape the noise and unwind from the stresses of city life. Shanghai has options for all budgets from luxury 5-star hotel spas to neighbourhood clinics and massage centres dispensing no-frills versions of age-old Chinese remedies. With branches throughout the city, the popular **Dragonfly** chain offers well-priced body and foot massages along with other revitalising treatments (www.dragonfly.net.cn). *Other spas and treatment centres are listed on p.37, p.56 and p.76.*

Dine, drink and spend big at **Shanghai IFC**, the city's smartest **shopping hub**

Two of Pudong's smartest mega malls face off in the heart of Lujiazui, the east riverbank's glitzy commercial centre. **Shanghai IFC Mall**, which opened in 2010, occupies the central podium of Cesar Pelli's IFC twin towers. Enveloped in a signature scent and playing piped classical concertos, the six-level mall is home to multi-storey boutiques including Cartier, Ferragamo, Prada et al., as well as more affordable brands like Miss Sixty and Diesel. You can pick up picnic supplies at the excellent City Super(market) at LG2 on your way to Century Park (p.130).

Dining options include Cali-Japanese sushi at Haiku by Hatsune and Italian stunner Isola Bar & Grill. In addition to opulent dining rooms, the fourth floor restaurants are blessed with stunning terraces overlooking the frenetic consumer action below. Plenty of Japanese fast-food chains and coffee shops can be found on the lower levels.

Opposite the IFC is China's largest mall, **Superbrand Mall**. This heaving retail behemoth contains 13 storeys of high-street labels. More surprising inclusions are an Egyptian-themed Cineplex, KTV rooms and an ice-skating rink. Several cafes and bars fringe the mall on the ground level – Element Fresh is a great place to stop for a refreshing smoothie or head to Blue Frog for something stronger.

Shanghai IFC Mall; 8 Century Avenue; tel: 2020 7000; www.shanghaiifc. com.cn; map G4
Super Brand Mall; 168 Lujiazui Road West; tel: 6887 7888; www.superbrandmall.com; map G4

125

Savour **local Chinese cuisine** and exquisite **river views**

Combining a fine Chinese meal with a side serving of Huangpu river views makes for a memorable gourmet experience. Fortunately, several popular local restaurants have outposts in Pudong's riverside malls.

Shanghai Min (9/F, Super Brand Mall; tel: 3208 9777) started as a small local diner with just four tables in 1987. It now has more than 30 restaurants across Asia serving upscale Shanghainese cuisine. Tasty dishes to choose on the encyclopedic menu include the Organic Vegetable Salad with Secret Sauce, Chicken Marinated with Chinese Rice Wine and Grandma's Meat Pot.

Taiwanese diner **Din Tai Fung** (*pictured*; Rm 24, 3/F, Super Brand Mall; tel: 5047 8882) serves

well-executed Chinese favourites in a bright, airy dining room with large windows looking out to Pudong. Be sure to order their signature pork and crabmeat *xiaolongbao* dumplings – or if you're feeling extra fancy, go for the delicious truffle version.

South Beauty (10/F, Superbrand Mall; tel: 5047 1917) is another gourmet emporium with designer dining rooms across the city. This outpost is beautifully styled with emerald green glass, striking scarlet armchairs, water channels and an open kitchen specialising in refined Sichuan and Cantonese cuisine. The wraparound 10th-floor river views are as jaw-dropping as the food is tongue-numbingly spicy.

If you prefer the flavours of Canton, **Lei Garden** (3/F, Shanghai IFC Mall, 8 Century Avenue; tel: 5106 1688) is a branch of the Michelin-star winning Hong Kong institution. Order top-sellers like the baby duck and speciality soups a day in advance. Roasted meats and superb dim sum are other reasons to go – and of course views over Lujiazui from the third floor.

Super Brand Mall and Shanghai IFC Mall: map G4. See p.125 for details

Visit China's answer to the Eiffel Tower: the **2010 World Expo China Pavilion**

From London's Crystal Palace, built to host the first Great Exhibition in 1851, to the Eiffel Tower in Paris in 1889 and the Brussels Atomium in 1958, through the ages, the World Fair has bequeathed its hosts with notable structures – the most outstanding of which become a symbol of that city.

Standing 63 metres (207ft) in height – three times the height of any other national pavilion – the bright red **China Pavilion** was the centrepiece of the 2010 World Expo, which garnered a record 73 million visitors. The China Pavilion itself received more than nine million visitors during the six-month long global showcase. While the majority of the Expo site – spanning both banks of the Huangpu River – is slated for redevelopment, a handful of core pavilions will endure, including the already iconic China Pavilion which remains a popular attraction, particularly for domestic tourists.

Officially nicknamed the 'Crown of the East', the pavilion design is notable for its traditional roof, said to represent an emperor's crown and made of interlocking *dougong* wooden brackets fixed layer upon layer

between the top of a column and a crossbeam. This style of architecture is said to date back more than 2,000 years. Fifty-six brackets were used in the pavilion roof to symbolise China's 56 minority ethnic groups. The roof was also fitted with 1,264 solar panels, making it China's largest single solar roof. Some visitors have suggested the building looks from a distance like a large Lego model.

The building closed in October 2011 for refitting, and is likely to reopen in early 2012. A World Expo 2010 Commemorative Exhibition opened in September 2011 in the Urban Footprint Pavilion and is expected to run for one year.

World Expo Site entrance on Xueye Road in Pudong; http://en.expo2010.cn; Tue–Sun 9am–5pm; charge; map B1

Zoom up the space-age **Oriental Pearl Tower** for a **360 degree view** from one of its spheres

Shanghai's skyline seems to change with startling regularity, but one city veteran has retained its iconic status since 1994. The development of the Pudong waterfront was still in its infancy when the Shanghai **Oriental Pearl Tower** opened after four years of construction. When completed, it was China's tallest building, although it has since been overtaken by a handful of urban skyscrapers – notably its near neighbour, the 101-storey Shanghai World Financial Centre. It is, however, the world's fourth tallest telecommunications tower, after the Canton Tower in Guangzhou, Toronto's CN Tower and Moscow's Ostankino Tower.

A series of gleaming silver and cranberry-coloured spheres are laced along the length of the 468-metre (1,535ft) TV tower, which is supported by three 7-metre (23ft) -thick stanchions – giving it the appearance of a space rocket on a launch pad. At night, the spheres are illuminated in electrifying neon kaleidoscopes. The main sightseeing platform is in a large sphere, 263 metres (863ft) above street level. Viewfinder plaques identify the skyline's standout structures to enhance the superb views. A second viewing level – the Space Module – sits in the upper sphere at 350 metres (1,092ft). Five smaller spheres contain a 25-room hotel, while the summit pearl has a rotating restaurant.

The **Shanghai Municipal History Museum** on the second level, features atmospheric recreations of cobble-stoned old Shanghai streets, a gun from the Opium Wars, and the original lions that sat in front of the Hong Kong and Shanghai Bank.

Oriental Pearl Tower; 1 Century Avenue; tel: 5879 1888; daily 8.30am–9.30pm; charge; map G5

Check out Arata Isozaki's feng shui-inspired
Himalayas Arts Centre

Pudong boasts many an experimental building, but lacks fine arts spaces. So the locally based Zendai Property Group decided to combine the two in one ambitious project. The owners of Pudong's acclaimed Zendai Museum of Modern Art have transferred the collection to the Himalayas Art Museum within the dramatic new **Himalayas Art Centre,** which it calls an 'archisculptural masterpiece for 21st century China'.

Japanese architect Arata Isozaki, famed for his work on the 1992 Barcelona Olympic Stadium and the Los Angeles Museum of Contemporary Art, designed the Himalayas Centre, which is infused with feng shui and eastern structural principles. Echoing elements of Gaudí's Modernist buildings in Barcelona, the uneven exterior design represents an 'organic forest'

of irregularly shaped holes carved into the walls rising from the ground to symbolise tree trunks.

The Himalayas Art Museum is scheduled to open in May 2012, with a collection that includes ancient Dunhuang frescoes, Yamato-e Japanese paintings based on China's Tang dynasty scroll-style art, oil paintings by contemporary artists and hand-painted Jingdezhen porcelain.

Also housed within this arresting building are the 1,100-seat DaGuan Theatre, an underground retail plaza, and the first Asia-Pacific hotel by Dubai luxury hotel group Jumeirah, in which every artwork, loaned from the owner's personal collection, is an original piece. Plus a rooftop 'infinity garden' and events stage.

Himalayas Art Centre; 1108 Meihua Road; www. himalayasart. cn; map G3

Ride a tandem, fly a kite or have a picnic with the locals in the beautifully landscaped **Century Park**

Although appearances may be deceptive, Shanghai isn't all about skyscrapers, elevated highways and apartment blocks. It's a surprisingly green city if you know where to look. **Century Park** is the largest public green space in the metropolitan area. Acting as a green lung for the city, it is a popular spot for biking, walking and relaxing amid the greenery. Anchored by a huge lake, this beautifully landscaped stretch of parkland rarely feels busy, even at weekends.

Designed by British landscaping firm LUC, Century Park blends Chinese and Japanese styles in the layout of its gardens, lakes and paths as well as grassland and wilderness.

Around the lake are several scenic spots, and the perimeter path is popular with joggers.

As well as plenty of attractive scenery to admire and landscapes to explore, the park offers a variety of recreational activities. Visitors can hire boats on the lake, or try their hand at tandem bike-riding along the wide paths and avenues (regular bikes are also available). If it's breezy enough, you can pick up a kite to fly at the park gates.

And if all that physical activity has you gasping for a drink or a bite to eat, there are convenience stores and teahouses dotted around the park.

Century Park; 1001 Jinxiu Road; tel: 5833 0221; daily 7am-6pm; map F-G3

Be a culture vulture at the **Oriental Arts Centre** or see who's on at the **Mercedes-Benz Arena**

Though proud of its space-age skyline, Pudong has long struggled with its perception as a cultural wasteland. All the cool culture occurred on the opposite side of the Huangpu River in Puxi. No longer. Two dramatically crafted performance centres are changing the way Shanghai views its east bank.

The **Oriental Arts Centre**, which opened in 2005, led Pudong's cultural charge. Designed by French architect Paul Andreu, it comprises five dark granite-based hemispheroids housing the lobby, performance hall, concert hall, exhibition hall and opera hall. Viewed from above, the building opens out like a flowering butterfly orchid. At night, 880 inlaid lights illuminate the roof to spectacular effect. The Oriental Arts Centre's acclaimed acoustics, contemporary design and varied performance spaces have attracted some of the world's leading philharmonic and chamber orchestras and opera performers. The Saturday brunch chorus and symphony concerts are a good-value way to experience this impressive venue.

In its former guise, the Expo Performance Centre hosted the spectacular opening and closing ceremonies for the 2010 World Expo. After Expo finished, the riverside venue was rechristened the **Mercedes-Benz Arena**, becoming China's first corporate naming rights deal for a major venue. The six-level, 18,000-seat arena stages concerts by Chinese and international popstars, theatrical and dance shows, and sporting events. Within the same complex are Shanghai's biggest ice rink, a six-screen cinema, a nightclub, restaurants and retail outlets. Like the Oriental Art Centre, this oyster-shell building is also radiantly lit at night.

Oriental Art Centre; 425 Dingxiang Road; tel: 6854 1234; www.shoac.com.cn; map F4
Mercedes-Benz Arena; 1200 Expo Avenue; tel: 400 181 6688; www.mercedes-benzarena.com; map B1

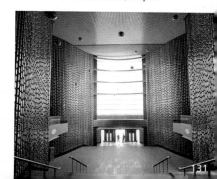

Dine on refined **Moroccan, Indian or Thai cuisine** or just **lounge on opium beds** sipping cocktails at **Face**

There was a time when Face, a heritage villa restaurant strung with lanterns and cushioned opium beds on the grounds of Ruijin Guesthouse, was *the* place to take visitors for a taste of Shanghai decadence. Since the Ruijin Guesthouse reclaimed the building, Face has moved to the magical grounds of the Dongjiao State Guesthouse in far-flung Pudong. Reassuringly far from the downtown crowds, it unites the cuisines of several countries in unforgettable surroundings.

Face is home to four separate restaurants, a cocktail lounge, a function space and a French patisserie. Each cuisine is cooked by expert chefs from that country.

If you're in the mood for Thai food, try **LanNa**. The seductive design and Southeast Asian antiques will transport you straight to Chiang Mai as you dine on aromatic curries and salads. If Indian is more your thing, head to **Hazara** (*pictured*). Located in an opulent free-standing tent on the formal lawn, it serves authentic North Indian fare that mixes nomadic flavours with courtly cuisine. Light Japanese fare prevails at **Syari**, where expert chefs roll and slice in a clean, minimalist environment. For North African food go to **El Wajh**, where the interior design resembles a cosy Marrakesh casbah. Sip mint tea after your meal and admire the terracotta and turquoise tones and tent ceilings.

Round off your meal with a cocktail at **Face Bar**. Enjoy the night breeze on the terrace, or lounge indoors on Qing dynasty daybeds. The **Visage Patisserie** next door is a good spot to pick up some pastries for breakfast the next day. Chef Eric Perez creates fanciful bites using ingredients imported from France.

Face; Dongjiao State Guesthouse, 1800 Jinke Road; tel: 5027 8261 3668; www.facebars.com; daily noon–2am; map H3, off map

Indulge your little emperors with Pudong's array of **child-friendly attractions**

Pudong is a vast residential district and home to Shanghai's finest schools which means it's a family-friendly place with plenty of activities on offer for kids.

Opened in late 2010, the full-sized indoor **ice rink at the Mercedes-Benz Arena** (p.131) features a state-of-the-art sound system and colourful lighting effects. Adult-sounding but very kid-friendly the cavernous **Shanghai Science and Technology Museum** has many intriguing exhibits, including the World of Robots, Children's Rainbow Land and Space Navigation, plus an IMAX cinema. Nearby, **Century Park** (p.130) is a popular spot for family kite flying, rollerblading and Frisbee throwing at weekends.

On the riverside in front of the Oriental Pearl Tower, the **Shanghai Ocean Aquarium** takes you on an underwater journey via the icy tides of the Antarctic, the rivers of Africa and the rainforests of Southeast Asia. En route you'll encounter sharks, Chinese water dragons, electric eels and jellyfish.

For a sweet treat, visit the extraordinary candy counter at the Pudong Shangri-La's **Yi Café** buffet restaurant. The dessert selection is vast, and kids can also pick up a special sweetbox and fill it with their own colourful pick-and-mix confectionery.

Shanghai Science and Technology Museum; 2000 Century Boulevard; tel: 6854 2000; www.sstm.org.cn; Tue–Sun 9am–5.15pm; charge; map F3
Shanghai Aquarium, 1388 Lujiazui Ring Road; tel: 5877 9988; www.sh-soa.com; 10am–6pm; charge; map H5
Yi Café; 2/F, Pudong Shangri-La, 33 Fucheng Road; tel: 5877 5372; www.shangri-la.com; map G4

Suzhou Creek and Northern Districts

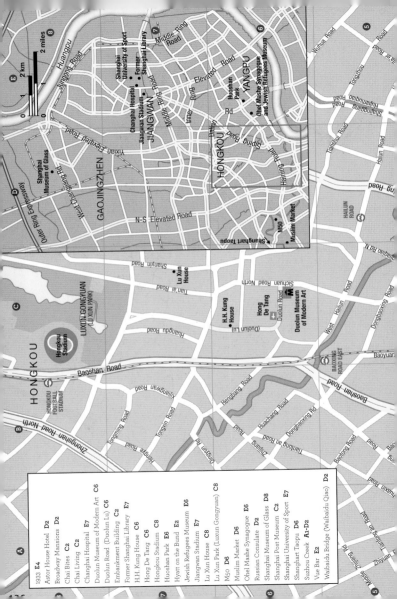

Map legend:

- 1933 **E4**
- Astor House Hotel **D2**
- Broadway Mansions **D2**
- Chai Bites **C2**
- Chai Living **C2**
- Changhai Hospital **E7**
- Duolun Museum of Modern Art **C6**
- Duolun Road (Duolun Lu) **C6**
- Embankment Building **C2**
- Former Shanghai Library **E7**
- H.H. Kung House **C6**
- Hong De Tang **C6**
- Hongkou Stadium **C8**
- Huoshan Park **E6**
- Hyatt on the Bund **E2**
- Jewish Refugees Museum **E6**
- Jiangwan Stadium **E7**
- Lu Xun House **C8**
- Lu Xun Park (Luxun Gongyuan) **C8**
- M50 **D6**
- Muslim Market **D6**
- Ohel Mashe Synagogue **E6**
- Russian Consulate **D2**
- Shanghai Museum of Glass **D8**
- Shanghai Post Museum **C2**
- Shanghai University of Sport **E7**
- Shanghai Taopu **D6**
- Suzhou Creek **A1-D2**
- Vue Bar **E2**
- Waibaidu Bridge (Waibaidu Qiao) **D2**

Map labels:

HONGKOU

HONGKOU FOOTBALL STADIUM

Hongkou Stadium

LUXUN GONGYUAN (LU XUN PARK)

GAOJINGZHEN

JIANGWAN

HONGKOU

YANGPU

Shanghai University of Sport
Former Shanghai Library
Middle Ring Road
Shanghai Library
Changhai Hospital
Jiangwan Stadium
Shanghai Museum of Glass
Huoshan Park
Ohel Mashe Synagogue and Jewish Refugees Museum
N-S Elevated Road
Shanghai Taopu
Muslim Market
M50
Lu Xun House
H.H. Kung House
Hong De Tang
Duolun Museum of Modern Art
Sichuan Road North
Baoshan Road
Baoyuan
BAIXING ROAD EAST

Roads: Jingong Road, Huangpu, Yixian Elevated Road, West Changjiang Rd, Outer Ring Expressway, Middle Ring Road, Elevated Road, Inner Ring, Guiping Road, Haining Road, Siping Road, Shanyin Road, Tian'ai Road, Huangu Road, Shanyin Road, Duolun Road, West Hailun Road, Hailun Road, Tangshan Road, Haliun Road, Tianshui Road, HAILUN ROAD, Baoshan Road North, Zhongshan Road North, Tongxin Road, Hengbang Road, Jiangwan Road, Tongzhou Road, Yuhua Road, Baotou Road, Middle Zhizhu Road, Zhongzhou Road, Tonghe Road, Dongbaoxing Rd, Guangling Road, Tongzhou Road, Tianbao Road, Huachang Road, Linping Road, Dongbaoxing Road, Dongjiangdong Road, Huajiangdong Road, Shangcheng Road, Zhenglan Rd N

Scale: 0 2 km, 0 2 miles, 0 1 2

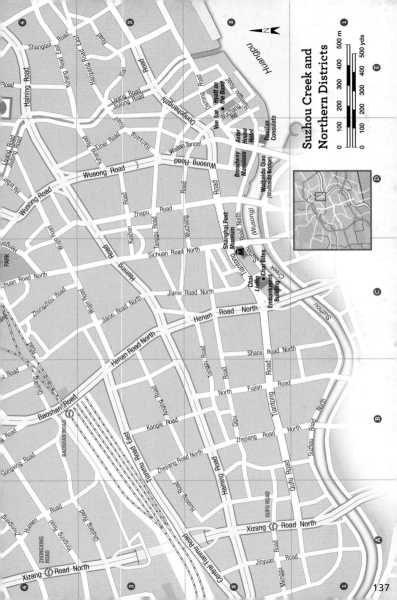

Suzhou Creek and Northern Districts

Follow the **literary trail** along Duolun Road, 1930s intellectual hub and home to revered writer, **Lu Xun**

Hongkou district was home to several progressive Chinese writers, artists and intellectuals, who settled around Duolun Road in the 1930s. Most famous of all was Lu Xun (1881–1936), a writer, thinker and revolutionary who is regarded as the father of modern Chinese literature. He was instrumental in founding the League of Leftist Writers in 1930 to 'struggle for proletarian liberation' through writing. The league is commemorated with a small museum in one of the writer's well-preserved houses.

Lu Xun lived out his final years in Hongkou and his legacy is writ large. His plain red-brick Japanese Concession house

has been left just as it was when he lived here. **Lu Xun Park** – a delightful green space with lakes, pagodas, and hordes of locals that gather to sing opera and play chess – also contains the writer's tomb, with memorial calligraphy inscribed by Mao Zedong, and the Lu Xun Memorial Hall exhibiting his letters, personal artefacts and photos from the period.

The L-shaped pedestrian stretch of **Duolun Road**, designated a 'cultural street' by the government, is lined with galleries, bookshops, teahouses, antique stores and several heritage buildings, along with bronze statues of famous residents in various states of writerly repose. Highlights of the street include the Hong De Tang, a church built in 1928 with upturned Chinese eaves and red columns, the proud Xi Shi Zhong Lou bell tower, and state-run Shanghai Duolun Museum of Modern Art (which pales in comparison to the independent M50 galleries, *p.142*). Stop for a look at the lavish Moorish-style house at the end of Duolun Road, built in 1924, for financier HH Kung.

Lu Xun Park: map C8
Duolun Road Cultural Celebrities Street: map C6

Visit the ghosts of Shanghai's Jewish past at the wartime Ghetto and **Jewish Refugees Museum**

Amazingly, there is no other place in the world that saved so many Jewish lives during World War II as Shanghai. Between 1938 and 1940, some 20,000 Jews flooded into the city, which had no visa restrictions at that time.

Shanghai's Jewish presence dates back to the 19th century. Sephardic Jewish families such as the Sassoons, Kadoories and Ezras became powerful developers of real estate, hotels, banking and infrastructure, setting Shanghai on track towards its 'Pearl of the Orient' status. They were followed by Russian Jews in the early 20th century, who arrived via the trans-Siberian rail line and formed a sizeable Ashkenazi community complete with Jewish hospitals, synagogues, restaurants and fur shops. The last group of Jewish immigrants to arrive in the city were German, Austrian and Polish refugees. Unfortunately, their arrival coincided with that of the Japanese. During World War II, these 'stateless refugees' were ordered into a two square-kilometre 'designated area' in Hongkou district, known as the Shanghai Jewish Ghetto.

The stone tablet at the entrance to Huoshan Park is Shanghai's only public monument to the area's historic role as a Jewish safe-haven. From the park, walk down Zhoushan Road to Changyang Road, once the main street of the ghetto. There are still a few plaques and symbolic details remaining on house walls and down narrow alleys. Still standing at number 62 is the **Ohel Moshe Synagogue**, founded by Russian Jews in 1927. The small **Jewish Refugees Museum** on the third floor serves as a memorial to the refugees and their ties to Shanghai.

For a deeper insight into Shanghai's Jewish history, Israeli documentarian Dvir Bar-Gal hosts minutely-researched walking tours held daily in English or Hebrew (www.shanghai-jews.com).

Shanghai Jewish Refugees Museum; 62 Changyang Road; tel: 6512 6669; daily 9am–5pm; charge; map E6

139

Step into **1933**, a former abattoir and **Art Deco masterpiece**

Art Deco was Shanghai's signature style: the streamlined elegant look, born at the Exposition for the Decorative Arts in Paris in 1925, was a metaphor for the new age of skyscrapers, steamships, trains and all things *moderne*. Progressive Shanghai embraced it eagerly, but made it her own by adding Chinese elements.

Art Deco defined the city skyline between the late 1920s and '40s, and permeated virtually all design, industrial buildings included. Built in 1933, the old Shanghai Abattoir became Asia's most prolific slaughterhouse. The sloping concrete bridges criss-crossing the conical interior were noted not just as supremely functional for the mass transportation of cattle, but also as an era-defining example of industrial design. Sat imperiously beside a meandering creek, with its geometrically precise Art Deco lines, squares and portholes, the imposing stone exterior of the building deliberately suggested a Bund-front municipal office, bank or cultural centre, rather than a meat-processing plant.

After ceasing meatpacking operations, the building was converted into a medicine factory in 1970 before later falling into disrepair. The new century brought a local government-commissioned restoration of the abattoir and a handful of adjacent structures. Reopened in 2007 as a 'creative lifestyle hub', the renamed 1933 development has not really found its feet – partially due to bad management and an out-of-centre location. A handful of shops and restaurants occupy its varied spaces, but a visit to witness this fine piece of industrial art – especially the restored roundhouse upper level, which is used as a creative events space (*pictured*) – is more than merited.

1933; 10 Shajing Road; www.1933 shanghai.com; map E4

Take a shine to the **Shanghai Museum of Glass**

Located in the dramatically restyled Shanghai Glass Factory in the northern manufacturing district of Baoshan, the Shanghai Museum of Glass, opened in 2011, is one of China's most original modern museums.

Glass is a predominant element in Shanghai's 21st-century skyline. This, plus the city's role as China's high-tech glass hub, was the inspiration for the Shanghai Glass Company to commission a museum outlining the contrasting timelines of glass technology and arts in Asia and the West. Designed in spacy black with copious glass panelling and colourful reflective lighting, it takes visitors on a superbly curated journey from ancient Egypt through the Middle Ages and China's Tang and Song dynasties to 21st-century glass applications used in China's space programme.

Video clips and installations showcase the role of glass design and technology in everything from the *24* television series to Barack Obama's Presidential acceptance speech and the seabed dredging of crystal treasures from the Titanic.

The highlight of the museum is its collection of glass art and sculpture from around the world displayed on the third floor balcony. From Baccarat's *Nuclear Pomegranate* to Mossi vases inspired by Lalique and Chinese artist Shan Shan Sheng's Bamboo Forest installation created from hand-blown Murano glass from Italy, this is real crystalline class.

685 Changning Road West; tel: 6618 1970; www.shmog.org; Tue–Sun 9.30am–4.30pm, until 9pm on Sat ; map D8

Seek out **cutting-edge Chinese art** at the funky warehouse galleries of **M50**

Over the last decade or so, the clusters of deserted mills along Suzhou Creek have become a fertile breeding ground for Shanghai's contemporary art community. Artists and bohemian types flocked to this once-seedy neighbourhood, attracted to the large, bright factory and warehouse spaces and low rents.

The largest of these artists' enclaves is M50, a funky catch-all name given to the collection of galleries in the former Xinhe Cotton Mill, at 50 Moganshan Road. M50 is the hub of the Chinese contemporary art boom in Shanghai, and is home to hundreds of artists' studios and professional galleries. Just a few years ago, these Concession-era warehouses were dilapidated spaces. Today they have been reinvented and many of the galleries – and the artists – have taken on a sophisticated veneer that can only come from selling expensive art.

A stroll through the galleries, which carry everything from well-known artists to newbies, photography to installation,

SHANGHART TAOPU

Shanghai's art community is now venturing even further afield in pursuit of affordable and intriguing gallery space. One of the latest enclaves to emerge is Shanghart Taopu. Billed as a warehouse style art museum, the unmissable zig-zag shaped red building offers a bright showroom exhibiting large installation and sculptural works, a café selling art books and products, plus an original archival room of Chinese contemporary art. Surrounding the gallery are several artist's workshops. Act like a collector and you may be allowed to poke your head in and meet the creators.

18 Wuwei Road; tel: 3632 2097; Wed–Sun 10am–6pm; map D6

is a free tour of Chinese contemporary art that is better curated, and more current than at any museum.

Excellent galleries to look out for include Italian-Chinese **Aike Gallery** (2/F, Building 1; tel: 5252 7164; www.dearco.it) which has a sister gallery in Palermo; **Vanguard Gallery** (Building 4; www.vanguard gallery.com) which focuses on the new works of emerging artists; and **OV Gallery** (Room 207; tel: 5465 7768; www.ovgallery.com) known for its fearless thematic exhibitions targeting contemporary social issues in China.

Two of M50's pioneering galleries are also still going strong. Initiated in Shanghai in 1996, **ShanghART** (Building 16; tel: 6359 3923; www.shanghartgallery. com) has become one of the country's most influential art institutions and has taken a lead in representing Chinese artists

on the international stage. Its soaring gallery is complemented by the neighbouring H Space, which hosts large installations and exhibitions.

Also commanding a sprawling warehouse space, **Eastlink** (5/F, Building 6; tel: 6276 9932; www. eastlinkgallery.cn) champions the work of China's innovative experimental artists.

For those interested in photographic art **Ofoto Gallery** (www.ofoto-gallery.com) presents cutting-edge photography in a sprawling series of rooms beneath an exposed loft ceiling.

Further down the road at 97 Moganshan Road, **M97** (tel: 6266 1597; www.m97gallery.com) is another exciting venue for art photography enthusiasts.

M50; 50 Moganshan Road; most galleries open daily 10am–6pm; map D6

Saunter across **Waibaidu Bridge** and between the **landmark buildings** at its northern end

Cross into Hongkou the old-fashioned way, over **Waibaidu Bridge** which spans the Suzhou Creek – and much of its history. When it was completed in 1908, the bridge (known then by the English as Garden Bridge) was only expected to last 40 years. More than a century later, it still carries traffic across Suzhou Creek to Hongkou district, where the late 19th-century American settlement was located.

Built at the confluence of Suzhou Creek and the Huangpu River, China's first steel bridge replaced earlier wooden bridges and allowed the International Settlement along the Bund to expand northwards.

During the Japanese Occupation, the bridge served as the demarcation line between occupied Hongkou and the International Settlement; it was guarded by turbaned Sikh policemen from the British forces on the Bund side and Japanese soldiers on the occupied side.

In 2009, a century after its construction, the entire bridge was floated to a downstream workshop for restoration and reinforcement to ensure that it can continue to carry motor and pedestrian traffic for decades to come. Today, the bridge is a great vantage point for views of Pudong to the east and the Suzhou Creek to the west.

SUZHOU CREEK NORTH BANK

The Victorian building at the northern end of Waibaidu Bridge is the **Astor House Hotel** – once one of Shanghai's most elegant hotels. Opened in 1911, it attracted the illustrious likes of Charlie Chaplin and Albert Einstein. The hotel is a little less exclusive these days (p.179), but the interior has so far been spared modernisation making a wander across creaky antique teak floors and through the high-ceilinged corridors hung with sepia photos of famous guests, particularly enchanting. On the third floor, the vaulted Tudor-style hall holds a mini museum of hotel artefacts.

Sat beside the water's edge next to Astor House, is the **Russian Consulate**. Dating back to 1916, it appears from the river like a luxury Soviet-era dacha. Today, the Russian Federation is the only country still occupying its original Shanghai consulate building.

Diagonally opposite, the cigar-coloured **Broadway Mansions** looms large. The 19-storey building was built as a luxury serviced apartment block in 1934, its bold Art Deco form taking in the full panorama of the Bund. It is best remembered as the wartime Foreign Correspondents Club, which occupied the top six floors. Since 1951 it has operated as a state-run hotel – and little of the period interior has survived.

Continue along Suzhou Creek, beyond the imposing **Shanghai Post Office** (*p.151*) to the **Embankment Building**, designed by prolific architects Palmer & Turner for Victor Sassoon in 1932. The streamlined dove-grey Art Deco complex was the largest apartment building in the Far East, with wide balconies, eight elevators, and servants' quarters for most apartments. It even had its own artesian well providing fresh water for the residents and the heated swimming pool.

Today, several of the huge apartments have been wonderfully restored. At **Chai Living** (www.chai living.com), you can book a short stay in one of these artistically renovated apartments with superb city views. Spanish tapas and cocktails are served at **Chai Bites** (tel: 3603 3511) downstairs.

Astor House Hotel; 15 Huangpu Road; tel: 6324 6388; map D2
Broadway Mansions; 20 Suzhou Road North; map D2
Embankment Building; 400 Suzhou Road North; map C2

Discover the secrets of **Chiang Kai-shek's 'new city'**, a fusion of Art Deco and Ming-dynasty design

During the 1930s, China's ruling Kuomintang Nationalist government devised a 'grand plan' to build a 'new Shanghai' civic centre in the northern Jiangwan district, far removed from the city's foreign concessions. When Chiang Kai-shek's Nationalists were defeated by Mao's Communists in 1949, the grandiose 'new city' plan was abandoned. The buildings that remain are classic examples of the fusion of Art Deco and Ming Chinese styles, and worth a detour.

A short walk from Xiangyin Road metro station (Line 8, Exit 4), what was built in 1935 as the Shanghai Museum is Building 10 of the **Changhai Hospital**. The museum's grand central hall is a patient waiting room, but you can wander in to glimpse the original paintwork and mosaics. Close by, Building 12 is the former Aviation Society Building, designed in

the shape of an Art Deco-styled aeroplane. Opposite the hospital, in the campus grounds of the **Shanghai University of Sport**, is the former City Hall. The impressive palace-like structure is now a campus administrative building, but visitors are permitted to explore the brightly decorated corridors.

One structure still used for its original purpose is Jiangwan Stadium. It was the largest in east Asia when it was completed in 1935 with a capacity of 40,000. Jiangwan Stadium metro station (Line 10) is a short walk from here.

Changhai Hospital; 168 Changhai Road; map E7
Shanghai University of Sport; 345 Changhai Road; map E7
Jiangwan Stadium; 346 Guohe Road; tel: 5522 4216; map E7

Stock up on textiles and tuck in to **lamb kebabs** at the **Friday Muslim Market**

Stroll along Changde Road on a Friday afternoon and it's hard to believe you're in Shanghai. The aroma of paprika lamb kebabs fills the air, women in traditional costume sell dried fruit as men in white skull-caps emerge from the Huxi Mosque. Naan breads are lined up on carts ready to be devoured, and carpets hang from makeshift stands. This part of town is a haven for Shanghai's Muslims, most of whom come from the Uighur ethnic community. More Turkic than Han, the Uighur people hail from Xinjiang Province in China's far west. Other Chinese Muslims are from the Hui ethnic minority, but all worship side by side at the Huxi Mosque.

Every Friday at around 11am, vendors begin to set up shop along a single block of Changde Road opposite the mosque. When prayers finish at 1pm, the market bustles with life. Get there at around midday to soak up the atmosphere, and snag the best lamb kebabs hot off the grill. Xinjiang Province is famous for its lamb dishes, especially *yangrou chuan* skewers, made with juicy chunks of mutton interspersed with fat from the tail. These cost just a handful of yuan

each, and go well with naan bread and an iced yoghurt drink.

The market has been bustling for around six years, but the first Huxi Mosque dates to 1914 when Muslims from rural provinces arrived in Shanghai. The current mosque was built in 1992 and has a two-storey prayer hall. The Friday market is a lynchpin of the city's Muslim community, and a chance for Uighur people to dress in their traditional costume, meet up with friends and sell the wares of their home province.

Muslim Market; Corner of Changde Road and Aomen Road; Fri 11am–mid-afternoon; map D6

Explore the **meandering Suzhou Creek** by boat or on foot with an **expert guide**

Shanghai's secondary waterway, **Suzhou Creek** (also known as Wusong River) runs 125km (78 miles) inland from the Huangpu River to Lake Tai. Historically, it was a commercial barge route transporting goods from the Shanghai docks to neighbouring cities. During the booming 1930s, warehouses, factories and glamorous residences sprang up along its meandering banks. By the end of the century, however, the water was heavily polluted and the area badly neglected. A multi-million dollar clean-up operation was launched in the mid-1990s to restore Suzhou Creek as a place to live and work in. Art galleries and studios began occupying old warehouses, trendy office spaces and event venues were created

in derelict factories, and high-rise apartments emerged to the detriment of several historic neighbourhoods that were razed.

Today, Suzhou Creek merits a visit to see how this industrial hinterland has been relandscaped as part of Shanghai's greater urban plan. Some fine examples of 1930s residential and industrial architecture reside along both banks, and a series of fine bridges spans the river. As you head inland, don't forget to look back – the views of Pudong from 'The Creek' are superb.

To tour Suzhou Creek scenery by boat, 45-minute cruises (RMB100 round trip) run from the Danba Road and Changhua Road wharves. Night cruises run until 9.30pm.

PERSONALISED TOURS
Locally based author, historian and tour guide Peter Hibbard, MBE, has been researching Shanghai history since the mid-1980s, and is an expert on the Suzhou Creek district. He conducts personalised walking tours beginning at the Waibaidu Bridge *(pictured)* that take in unique riverside neighbourhoods and heritage buildings, and adds his own personal anecdotes from watching this area change over the last 25 years.
www.gingergriffin.com

Blow your mind and tastebuds at an exclusive 10-seat **molecular restaurant**

Set in a secret location beside Suzhou Creek, experimental eatery **Ultraviolet** is the brainchild of university chemistry major turned culinary inventor, Paul Pairet, the creative force behind the popular brasserie Mr & Mrs Bund (*p.32*). Ultraviolet is the French chef's dream project, designed to broaden the parameters of a restaurant meal and rethink the way our senses interact when we eat.

Pairet does this with a 20-course set menu, whereby each staged course is accompanied by a 'choreographed interplay of sensory components' – from projections and scent to music and mists. Catering to just 10 patrons a night, the high-tech dining room is wired with a light projection tracking system with infrared cameras able to follow

plates around the table, a dry scent diffuser wafting Givaudan aromas, and a panoramic screen showing immersive projections, from seascapes to 1950s wallpaper.

Imagine a gothic rock n' roll church scene with the faint scent of cathedral stone, ACDC's *Hells Bells* blasting and a nitro-frozen palate cleanser of apple wasabi that melts so fast it's served directly in the mouth – communion style. Other dishes that may feature on any given night include 'Encapsulated Bouillabaisse', a single Cuttlefish Noodle presented in a concentric circle, and Tomato Peach 'No Shark Fin' Soup – each presented with their own mind- and palate-bending scenarios. Expect to be wowed.

Ultraviolet; www.uvbypp.cc

Take a dip in a **sky-high Jacuzzi** and sip alfresco martinis at **Vue Bar**

Sited on the bend of the Huangpu River on the North Bund, atop the luxury Hyatt hotel *(p.176)*, **Vue** boasts a truly unique vista – staring straight down Shanghai's main artery, flanked to the right by the classical architecture of the Bund and to the left by the glassy futurism of Pudong. Spectacular by day, the panorama is truly sensational at night – especially from the rooftop Jacuzzi.

Vue is a multi-concept penthouse venue comprising a modern European restaurant designed like a private residence on the 30th floor of the Hyatt's West Tower, plus six private dining rooms on the 31st floor. The lounge action begins on the 32nd floor in Vue Bar. Styled by Japan's in-demand Super Potato interior design team, it features a wine cellar style entrance, exposed brick walls, fibre glass partitions and a circular bar surrounded by floor-to-ceiling glass to optimise the view.

So far so cool, but ascend a sweeping staircase to the 33rd floor for the *pièce de résistance*. The stairway opens out onto a roofless deck terrace offering comfy day-beds, a resident DJ – and a circular Jacuzzi for sipping Vue-tini cocktails and sightseeing in sync. The stunning views and breezy deck make this a hot Sunday afternoon spot for post-brunch lounging. In the evenings, Shanghai's beautiful people sip and splash as the city around them dazzles in neon. And don't worry if you have forgotten your swimming gear – 'Vue Jacuzzi Wear' can be ordered from the bar menu.

Hyatt on the Bund; 199 Huangpu Road; tel: 6393 1234 ext 6348 (lounge), ext 6328 (restaurant); www.shanghai.bund. hyatt.com; map E2

Come face to face with a Greek god on **Shanghai's Post Office** tower

Occupying a prime site at the north end of the Sichuan Road Bridge on the banks of Suzhou Creek is the **Shanghai Post Office**. Built in 1924, it handled foreign mail for all 48 nationalities officially represented in Shanghai at the time, and is still the city's main post office today.

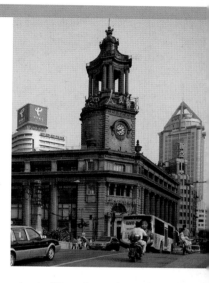

The stately stone building, encompassing an entire city block, is fronted by Corinthian columns and topped by a bronze capped Baroque bell tower. The interiors of the main postal hall are just as impressive, decorated with original black and white mosaic tiling, carved wooden service windows and handsomely coffered ceilings.

Pass through the operational postal hall to the newly renovated **Shanghai Post Museum** (Wed, Thur, Sat, Sun 9am–5pm; free) which charts the history of the Chinese postal system, from ancient beacon towers to modern mechanisation using interactive models, archival photographs and postal memorabilia.

When you've finished exploring the different exhibits (don't miss the precious stamp hall displaying postal stamp art across the decades), exit into the beautiful internal atrium courtyard and take the lift to the rooftop. The landscaped roof garden is the building's greatest asset, offering grassed-over areas, sensational views over Shanghai and a close-up look at the magnificent clock tower adorned with bronze statues of Greek gods Hermes, Eros and Aphrodite. Be sure to snap a photo from here of the futuristic Shanghai skyline, backset against the classical stone urns along the roof ledge.

Shanghai Post Office; 250 Suzhou Road North; daily 8am–10pm; tel: 6393 6666; map C2

Xuhui, Changning and Hongqiao

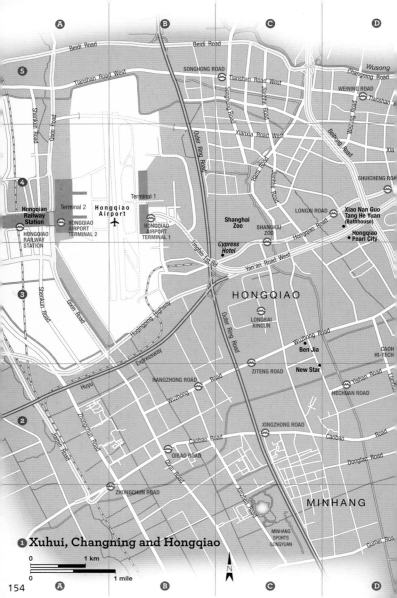

Xuhui, Changning and Hongqiao

155

Discover the **best little izakayas** and hidden shochu bars in **Japan-town**

In the 1990s, Japanese entrepreneurs poured into Shanghai, settling in the western suburbs. Two decades later, Hongqiao is a veritable Little Japan. Fukuoka ramen? Sumo wrestler hot pot? Fourth-generation tempura master? Shanghai has them all. None are as fun, however, as the izakaya, the uniquely Japanese blend of restaurant and pub.

You'll find **Toriyasu** (890 Changning Road; tel: 5241 1677; daily 5.30pm–1am; map E5) by its slatted-wood facade and sadistically small door. The menu flutters on paper strips tacked to the wall or comes hand-written in tiny Chinese characters. No matter. Sit in front of the smoky charcoal grill, the source of Toriyasu's magic, and point to what's cooking: butterflied chicken wings, thighs threaded with fat leeks, tomatoes wrapped in bacon. Wash it down with draft Asahi or small flask of sake, and remember to duck on the way out.

At **Tentekomai** (295 Wuyi Road; tel: 6212 9755; daily 5.30–11.30pm; map F5) a quaint izakaya, the door is normal-sized; it's the gyoza that is tiny. Snack on the one-bite dumplings before walking down the street to **Shanty** (84 Wuyi Road; tel: 6225 8635; daily 7.30pm–2am; map F5) the hush-hush shochu and plum bar of a resident Japanese trader. The Russian bartender, fluent in Japanese and English, will offer up suggestions (and, more rarely, a taste of her home-made borscht), but to snag one of the 14 seats, you'll have to swallow the RMB50 sitting fee.

Alternatively, that RMB50 will get you from leafy Wuyi Road to **Yamatoya** (459 Guyang Road; tel: 5477 5771; daily noon–2pm, 5.30–10.30pm; map E4) in a taxi, with enough change for a small bowl of oden, the featherlite Japanese stew that's on every table. The dark wood and stone vibe belies Yamatoya's izakaya soul, and what it lacks in smoke and general inebriation, it more than makes up for in roasted edamame and killer fried chicken.

Stock up on tea leaves at **Tianshan Tea City**

For a mall dedicated solely to caffeinated products, Tianshan Tea City is a remarkably calm place. Perhaps it's the influence of the faux-temple architecture. The halls of this three-storey tea emporium are lined with little shops specialising in everything from high-elevation Taiwanese oolongs to Hangzhou's Dragon Well green.

Head to the first floor for a lesson in the surrounding region's green tea types, which are among the best in the country. Small plates display the tight curls of Suzhou's *biluochun*, the paddle-like *Taiping houkui* ('monkey-picked'), and the flat blades of Hangzhou's *longjing* (Dragon Well), China's most famous green tea. Stop, sit, sniff, sip, say thank you, and move on. There are two more floors to go.

From the parking lot, ascend the escalator at the yellow sign. Turn left and pop into Wuyi Star (No. 2093) for their signature Fujianese oolong, *da hongpao* ('big red robe'), in colour-coded tins (white for fragrance, gold for flavour). Around the next corner, past the Yixing clay teapots, are the oval leaves of Liu'an *guapian*, an unusual green said to resemble melon seeds (No. 2053).

Prefer milk and sugar? Stall 2008 specialises in Keemun, a fruity black that's a prime ingredient in English breakfast tea. Don't do that to the expensive oolongs at No. 2076 though, plucked from the top of Taiwan's highest mountains, or the pricey discs of aged *pu'er*, a dark and smoky black from Yunnan that's the preserve of serious teaheads.

Casual drinkers should drop into Linzhiyu (No. 3028), a hip spot among the third floor's dusty curio stores, for the Hershey Kiss-sized *pu'er* samples and, surprisingly, wild honey from the young couple's Yunnan hometown.

Tianshan Tea City; 518 Zhongshan Road West; www.dabutong.com; daily 8.30am–8.30pm; map E5

Slip on a pair of **tropical pyjamas** and explore the kooky world of the **Chinese bathhouse**

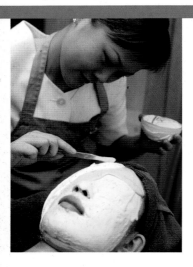

For the uninhibited, a Chinese bathhouse experience offers unforgettable cultural insights. A hangover from the days when most households didn't have showering facilities, a visit to the bathhouse remains popular. The modern-day variety has morphed into an all-in-one entertainment emporium, offering round-the-clock bathing, gaming, dining and more.

For good, clean family fun, try **Xiao Nan Guo Tang He Yuan** in Hongqiao. The bathhouse lobby resembles a retro five-star hotel, with chandeliers, a marble check-in counter and self-playing grand piano. Here the similarities end,

because patrons of this five-storey pleasure palace pad around in garish Hawaiian mumus – or nothing at all.

Leave your shoes (and modesty) at reception and head into the segregated changing rooms and bathing areas filled with unclothed bodies. Signage is in Chinese but it's easy to pick out the milk, 'green' and Japanese baths. Between dips, there's a cold plunge pool, steam room and sauna. After your soak, head to the communal scrubbing room for a 30-minute all-over body exfoliation (RMB48). An extra RMB20 earns you a facemask of cucumber pulp or a dousing in drinking milk.

After showering, it's time to towel off and pull on the regulation Hawaiian pyjamas to explore the rest of the emporium, where various rooms feature ping pong, snooker, mahjong and karaoke. If you're feeling hungry, multiple cafés serve restorative noodles and dim sum. Finish up at the huge foot massage area where reclining beds are fitted with mini TV screens. Save on a hotel and spend the night here if you wish!

Xiao Nan Guo Tang He Yuan; 3337 Hongmei Road; tel: 6465 8888; daily 11am–9am; charge; map D4

Select premium pearls and **design your own jewellery** at Hongqiao Pearl City

There's no better place to shop for pearls than China, which overtook Japan as the world's number one supplier in 2010. As Shanghai is located near to the freshwater pearling areas of China, they're particularly cheap and, with some 30 or so vendors, **Hongqiao Pearl City** offers better choice and prices than elsewhere in the town.

Located in the Japanese and Korean quarter of Shanghai, the market is in a mall in a shopping district dotted with anime bookshops and *bibimbap* (mixed rice with vegetables) restaurants. The mall itself is a garish 1990s construction and the bottom floor houses a fake goods market. On the second floor, however, is a relatively crowd-free pearl market absent of the usual onslaught of hawkers.

Expect to bargain hard – first-quoted prices can be triple or quadruple what you should pay. A pair of freshwater pearl earrings should cost RMB20 and strings of pearls around RMB200, though the bigger the pearls and more perfectly rounded, the costlier. For timeless pearl studs, **Daxi Pearl** at the top of the escalator couples friendly, English-speaking service with a good selection. If you feel creative, **Vicky Pearl** at G050 is one of the best places to customise your own jewellery. Staff speak English, and you can choose the type of chain, setting, pearl shape and colour, though note: only white, black, pink, lavender and peach naturally occur.

It's relatively easy to tell if a pearl is genuine by simply looking at it, but vendors are happy to do a 'scrape test' – where they tease tiny shards off the back of a pearl with a knife – to prove they're not painted plastic. A smudge of the thumb smoothes any potential scratches.

Hongqiao Pearl City; 3721 Hongmei Road; daily 10am–9pm; map D4

Explore the **manicured gardens** and ornamental lakes of Changning District's **state guesthouses**

While the metropolitan parks of the city centre can be less than relaxing (with crowds of people, loud music blaring, and odd rules governing where you can and can't venture), the beautiful state guesthouses of Changning District and their sprawling manicured grounds provide a more peaceful experience.

The **Hongqiao State Guesthouse** has one of the most beautiful green spaces in the city – a park that is rarely visited due to its somewhat hidden location. The five-star hotel is

part of the state-owned Donghu Hotels group, and became an official lodging house when Deng Xiaoping decided to create state guesthouses in the 1980s to accommodate visiting dignitaries. What makes Hongqiao State Guesthouse particularly special is the 50-acre green space surrounding it. The gardens are part of the former country estate of Sir Victor Sassoon, the British-Jewish real estate tycoon whose inner-city residence was under the copper dome of his most famous property, the Peace Hotel.

The land retains the charm of days gone by, with paths winding through forests, bamboo groves and carpets of bluebells in spring, and ornamental stone chairs where visitors can sit and soak up the atmosphere.

Sassoon's legacy also lives on in the **Cypress Hotel**, 5km (3 miles) to the southwest. The property's original Tudor-style mansion now forms building No. 1 of the Jinjiang-owned guesthouse.

Hongqiao State Guesthouse; 1591 Hongqiao Road; tel: 6219 8855; www. hqstateguesthotel.com; map E4 Cypress Hotel; 2419 Hongqiao Road; tel: 6322 3855; www. cypresshotelshanghai.cn; map C3

Paint the town at **contemporary art enclave**, Redtown

An old state-run steelworks in the west of the former French Concession is now a trendy arts district, typifying the metamorphosis that spawned lifestyle hubs like Xintiandi and Tianzifang. Known as Redtown, the complex started life as the Shanghai No. 1 Steel Factory in 1956. Nowadays, the main factory building has been converted into a cavernous art space, while the surrounding lanes are home to cafés, bars, galleries and shops.

Shanghai Sculpture Space (tel: 6280 5629; www.sss570.com) opened in 2005, and dominates Redtown with its giant 10,000-sq-meter (108,000 sq ft) indoor area (split into Halls A and B) and sprawling garden. A mix of permanent and temporary displays keeps things fresh. If you need a caffeine fix after browsing the installations, head to nearby **Beca Café** (Building C; tel: 6280 7232). Chic black furniture and a contemporary bohemian vibe form the backdrop for coffee, crêpes, cake and Western-style meals and snacks.

In the mood for some more art? Try the **Minsheng Art Museum** – another large-scale venue for showcasing the work of contemporary Chinese artists.

Stick around after night falls and witness the arrival of Shanghai's beautiful people at **Node Lounge** (tel: 5230 7366; www.nodelounge.com) – a club and bar frequented mainly by young Japanese residents of nearby Hongqiao. Node is popular for its trendy, minimalist decor, and for the spacious garden that's a perfect hang-out on warm evenings.

Redtown also contains **Club Hero**, a studio for muay Thai, Brazilian jiu-jitsu, boxing and Mixed Martial Arts (MMA), plus several clothing boutiques and cafés. Thanks to its position on the outskirts of the old French Concession, it is spared the crowds that turn Xintiandi and Tianzifang manic at weekends.

Redtown; 570 Huaihai Road West; map F4

Join the locals at a **Korean barbecue or bathhouse** in Hongqiao

When the world economy crashed in 2008, the collapse of the *won* sent many Korean expatriates in Shanghai packing. Longbai, once a thriving Koreatown, has yet to recover. Still, at any given time, you'll find scores of the remaining residents at one of two places: the bathhouse or the barbecue.

Obscured from the road by a Hyundai dealership, Seoul-import **Ben Jia** is Shanghai's finest Korean barbecue restaurant, not least for the overwhelming tray of fresh leaves and vegetables to wrap it all up in. Waiters hustle through the dining room with an endless parade of *banchan*, the customary *kimchi*, salads and sides, stopping to adjust the thinly sliced beef brisket (*samgyup*

chadol) on your charcoal fire, or deliver another Hite beer.

Around the corner is **New Star**, a family-friendly Korean-style bathhouse. It's a study in contrasts: heated floors and frozen beer mugs, steaming hot tubs and freezing 'shock' showers. Afterwards, head upstairs to the stone huts filled with restorative stones, and then – where else? – into the walk-in freezer.

A NORTH KOREAN NIGHT OUT

The food is nothing special, and the supposedly North Korean staff may be secretly Chinese, but for a rare glimpse into the hermit kingdom, Okryu does the trick. Tall beauties in traditional dress take orders for Pyongyang-style noodles from a curious Japanese and South Korean crowd. They then rush onstage to sing nostalgic Chinese songs and jam on accordions, tambourines and electric guitars. Show starts 7.30pm. *Pyongyang Okryu; 3/F, Jianguo Hotel, 439 Caoxi North Road; tel: 6481 1569; map F4*

Ben Jia; 1339 Wuzhong Road; tel: 5118 2777; daily 10am–11pm; map C3
New Star; 258 Jinhui South Road; tel: 3432 0777; open daily, 24 hours; map C2

Eat with the elite in a colonial villa setting at Fu 1088

Only the doormen mark out this colonial villa as a restaurant. Originally a residence of a powerful relative (whispered to be a Kuomintang general), the elegant mansion passed through owner Fu Yafen's family and managed to survive Shanghai's tumultuous history almost fully intact; the gorgeous Spanish tile and cherry-wood staircases are original and antiques fill the 17 rooms, where the film-set atmosphere meets chef Tony Lu's refined Shanghainese cooking.

Xunyu has emerged as Lu's calling card. Warm, fragrant, and the colour of dark mahogany, Fu 1088's version is a stack of river fish marinated in soy sauce, sugar, and rice wine before a light frying. He does as well with *hongshao rou*, succulent and melting red-braised pork belly, and cold 'drunken chicken', a speciality of nearby Shaoxing that uses that city's well-known rice wine as a marinade.

Shanghai's surrounds are crisscrossed by lakes and rivers, and it's from these waterways that the city's cuisine is drawn: 'crystal' river shrimp, sautéed with the leaves of Hangzhou's famous *longjing* tea, or a Reeves shad steamed in yellow rice wine and the region's Jinhua ham. Being able to serve this particular fish adeptly was once a test of a lady's upbringing in a house like this. These days, meeting the RMB300 minimum is all that's needed.

Fu 1088, 375 Zhenning Road; tel: 5239 7878; daily 11am–2pm, 5.30–11pm; map F5

Take a warp-speed trip on one of China's amazing 'bullet' trains

The ongoing expansion of airports and high-speed railways is transforming domestic travel in China. At the end of 2010, China had 8,358km (5,193 miles) of high-speed track in operation. The extent of the network is estimated to double to 16,000km (10,000 miles) by 2015.

Shanghai is leading the way for transport infrastructure upgrading. Its second airport, Hongqiao, welcomed a large new terminal in 2010, and was joined by a new railway station (*map A4*) for super-fast travel around China. Both the airport and rail station are easily accessed using Metro Line 2 from downtown.

Travelling at up to 390km/h (243mph) China's 'bullet' trains have slashed journey times, making excursions from Shanghai ever more appealing. The Unesco World Heritage-listed classical gardens of Suzhou are now just a 30-minute train ride away, and the mystical West Lake and tea plantations of Hangzhou take 50 minutes to reach. There's even a hi-speed train service linking Shanghai and the capital, Beijing – the 1,318km (819-mile) ride on a bullet train takes just 4 hours and 48 minutes.

Expansion plans include a proposed extension of the MagLev train to connect Pudong and Hongqiao airports. Under construction, the Hongqiao Commercial Hub – featuring a 420-room 'urban resort' hotel, luxury brand mall, fine Asian dining and a space-age performing arts centre – will be directly linked to Hongqiao airport and rail station.

Pay your respects to **early Communist martyrs** at one of Shanghai's most compelling monuments

Shanghai's revolutionary history is often packaged in hard-hitting state-speak that is heavy on rhetoric but less attentive to historic detail. The **Longhua Martyrs Memorial** Cemetery, while not short on pro-Communist hype, is a poignant reminder that amid the wordy political ideology, China's 20th-century social upheavals involved significant human pain and suffering.

The cemetery commemorates a tragic moment in Shanghai's history when hundreds of young Communists were killed during the Kuomintang's reign of terror. On 12 April 1927, these revolutionaries were rounded up and taken to the execution grounds in what was then the Longhua Garrison. Each April, Longhua's orchard of peach trees blossoms in remembrance.

The cemetery today is all meticulously landscaped gardens and high-tech fountains, with a blue-glass Louvre-esque pyramid and a Memorial Hall dedicated to the Communist martyrs. Outside an eternal flame burns in front of the *Tomb of the Unknown Martyrs*, sculpted by He Pan, which features a Herculean sculpture half-entombed in the lawn with an arm extending upward in hope. Dotted across the park other giant concrete socialist-realist statues depicting heroic revolutionary struggles against anti-Communist adversaries.

The Martyrs' Cemetery also features reconstructions of the Kuomintang prison and execution grounds, and a memorial museum that narrates (in English and Chinese) with images, videos and historical artefacts, the bloody revolutionary struggle after the founding of the Chinese Communist Party in 1921.

Longhua Martyrs Memorial Cemetery; Longhua Road West; daily 7am-4.30pm; free; map G3

Pair a **folk opera stage show** with a **fiery Sichuan feast**

Shunxing is a grand old teahouse chain from Chengdu, the capital of southwest China's Sichuan province. This bastion of laconic Sichuan culture recently arrived in China's most harried city. This being Shanghai, the colourful traditional wooden gateway is tacked on to an office tower, but what lies within is pure Sichuan.

The action in this elegant 1,000-seat restaurant – each one a hefty, carved wooden chair – is centered on a classic Sichuanese opera stage, and just edges out the kitchen's own deft performance. Every night at 7.30pm, the resident troupe upbraids each other in sing-song dialect, wails through a repertoire of countryside opera, and performs a mesmerising 'face-changing' routine with an endless cache of silk masks.

Sichuan's other art, of course, is the region's famously fiery food, exemplified by Shunxing's outstanding rendition of *mapo doufu*, silky cubes of tofu in a glistening red bath of chillies and numbing Sichuan peppercorns.

For a more genteel evening in Old Shanghai, head to **The Door**. On weeknights from 6.30–8pm, quiet young ladies play traditional Chinese instruments like the *erhu* and *pipa* in the former military warehouse, now done up in high 1920s style. The nostalgic, pre-war touch extends beyond the antique furniture to the waiters in long tunics, who glide over the parquet floor bearing classic Shanghainese and Cantonese dishes.

Shunxing; 2–3/F, 1088 Yan'an Road West; tel: 6213 8988; daily 11.30am–9.30pm – reserve for a stageside table; map F4
The Door; 1468 Hongqiao Road; tel: 6295 1717; daily 10.45am–2pm, 4–11.30pm; map E4

Take a look inside **Xujiahui Cathedral** and browse the atmospheric **Bibliotheca Zikawei**

Today, the bustling Xujiahui district houses cathedrals of commerce, but a century ago this part of Shanghai was deeply Catholic territory. In fact, Xujiahui is named after the Xu family, whose descendent, Paul Xu (born 1562), was the first Chinese high official to convert to Christianity. He bequeathed his estate to French Jesuits who, in 1847, built a monastic complex which included a seminary, orphanage, workshops, printing press, Latin library and weather observation station.

The centrepiece of the complex is China's largest Catholic church. Completed in 1906, **St Ignatius Cathedral** (Xujiahui Cathedral) is a dramatic vision of red brick, stained glass and towering spires, both toppled during the Cultural Revolution, when the cathedral was used as a grain store. Since then, the entire church has been restored and is once again used by the Catholic community. Take a peek inside the angel-white interiors and note the new stained glass panels, crafted by local nuns, incorporating modern Chinese symbolism and characters to illustrate the gospel stories.

The former priests' residence now houses the lovely **Bibliotheca Zikawei**, an incredible collection of rare books. The ground floor is designed in the style of a classic Qing library, while the beautiful upper floor is a fine copy of the Vatican Library. Breezy Italianate corridors, dark wood staircases and an atmospheric reading room make for delightful browsing.

St Ignatius Cathedral; 158 Puxi Road; tel: 6438 2595; open for public viewing Sat–Sun 1-4.30pm; map F4
Bibliotheca Zikawei; 80 Caoxi Road North; tel: 6487 4095; free 15-min library tours on Sat 2-4pm; map F4

Unwind in the serene retreat of **Guilin Park**

In a high-density city like Shanghai, public parks and gardens provide welcome havens of solitude, space and social interaction. Chinese horticulturalists have long been experts at cultivating gorgeous Zen gardens. One of Shanghai's finest is **Guilin Park**. This charming walled garden was once the private residence of a not-so charming character – Huang Jingrong, or 'Pockmarked Huang', a notorious gangster who doubled up as head of police in the French Concession. The home and garden was completed over four years in the early 1930s.

Pay the RMB2 entrance fee to access this popular park landscaped with pagodas, grottoes, rockeries and century-old cypress and pine trees. The outer and inner gardens are separated by an undulating stone wall that was designed to resemble a dragon's back.

If you visit around September you are in for a special treat. The name Guilun Park refers to the more than 1,000 sweet *gui* (osmanthus) trees planted throughout. When the tiny cream flowers bloom at the first signs of autumn, the whole park is draped with an intoxicating fragrance.

SHANGHAI BOTANICAL GARDEN
Not far from Guilin Park is the **Shanghai Botanical Garden**, an 80-hectare collection of multiple species of magnolias, peonies, azaleas, Chinese orchids, rhododendron, bamboo, maples and more.
1111 Longwu Road; tel: 5436 3369; www.shbg.org; map G1

The central Four Religion Hall is now a rustic teahouse. Pick your leaves and you'll be supplied with a large thermos of hot water. While away the afternoon on the ornately carved verandah sipping tea and watching senior citizens practice opera in the gardens and couples posing for Western-style pre-wedding pictures.

Guilin Park; 128 Guilin Road; map E2

Visit the final resting place of **Soong Qingling**, one of China's most powerful women

The story of the three Soong sisters is one of the most compelling in modern Chinese history, and this peaceful park is a great place to learn about their lives while escaping the noise and bustle of central Shanghai. The Mausoleum of Soong Qingling contains a foreign cemetery, a museum, lush parkland and a children's activity area plus the final resting place of Qingling and her parents.

Soong Qingling (1893–1981) was one of the most powerful women in Chinese history, ruling the country alongside her husband, Dr Sun Yat-sen. Out of the three sisters, Qingling is remembered for her love of power. The eldest, Ailing, married Guomindang finance minister and millionaire H.H. Kung, garnering her a reputation for loving money. The youngest, Meiling, was the wife of Kuomintang leader Chiang Kai-shek, and is noted for her dedication to her country. The charismatic Soong Qingling, the only one of the influential Soong sisters to remain in China, is commemorated at this tranquil site in Shanghai's Changning district.

The Soong family plot is part of the Wan Guo cemetery that is also the resting place of patriots, war heroes and over 600 foreigners from 25 countries. The centrepiece is Qingling's gravesite, with a white marble statue in her likeness. To the left is the final resting place of Lin Yan'e, Qingling's nanny and lifelong friend.

The **Soong Qingling Exhibition Hall** contains over 500 photographs and artefacts that offer insights into China's political and social history during the most turbulent periods of the 20th century.

Soong Qingling's Mausoleum;
21 Songyuan Road; tel: 6474 7183;
daily 8.30am–5pm; map E4

hotels

Since the early 20th century, Shanghai's hotel scene has influenced the city's architectural, social and economic development. Back in the 1930s, the 'Paris of the Orient' epitomised modern sophistication with glamour-laden retreats like the Cathay, Palace, Astor House and Park hotels – inspired in style and substance by New York, London and Paris – which attracted global travellers plus local high society to stay and play.

After a long hiatus following World War II and Mao's Communist revolution, the 1990s sparked a renaissance in Shanghai hospitality, with internationally branded business abodes springing up citywide. This continued into the new millennium, as luxury hotel clusters decorated the Lujiazui, People's Square, Nanjing Road and Hongqiao skylines – many boasting prices as elevated as the high-rise room levels, plus sophisticated dining and deluxe spas.

The pace of development remains unrelenting. High-profile architects and wealthy developers are teaming up to reconstruct the Pudong and Puxi landscapes with glassy 'mixed use' skytowers, comprising hotels, retail and office space. At the same time, heritage properties along the Bund and in the former French Concession are being converted into more atmospheric, period-infused boutique hotels, while cutting-edge contemporary interiors define a growing band of small design-led hotels.

None of these come cheap, of course. Shanghai is an expensive place to bed down and demand for accommodation still outstrips supply, so book early. Visitors on a lower budget need not fear, however. Shanghai also boasts Asia's fastest growing budget hotel portfolio, most of which are well located and can be booked online.

HOTEL PRICES
Price for an average room in high season, including breakfast

$$$$ over RMB2,000
$$$ RMB1,500–2,000
$$ RMB750–1,500
$ under RMB750

Historic

Fairmont Peace Hotel
■ The Bund

20 Nanjing Road East; tel: 6321 6888; www.
fairmont.com/peacehotel; map p.24 D5; $$$

Sir Victor Sassoon's glorious Art Deco palace on the Bund reopened in 2010 after a no-expense-spared renovation which retained many of the exquisite interior details. Standard guestrooms are a tad small, so push the boat out and upgrade to a grand Nine Nations Suite with a river view. Live music in the Jazz Bar is a star attraction.

Mansion Hotel
■ French Concession

82 Xinle Road; tel: 5403 9888; www.china
mansionhotel.com; map p.93 E4; $$$

Built and owned by a pre-War Shanghai gangster, this walled mansion has been repurposed as a 1920s-themed hotel. Many of the large, classically decorated rooms feature spacious stone terraces overlooking the courtyard. Opium pipes, gramophone records, old photos and other artefacts of the period are exhibited in the lobby lounge. The top-floor terrace bar looks out over mid-town Shanghai.

@ Gallery Suites
■ French Concession

525 Hengshan Road; tel: 5179 5000; www.
artgalleryhotels.com; map p.92 D2; $$

Housed in a 1930s mansion once owned by a Russian princess, this atmospheric hotel is charmingly decorated with period Shanghai-deco detailing. The generously sized rooms feature Art Deco furnishings, claw-footed bathtubs and timeless photos of old Shanghai, combined with all the modern comforts.

Waldorf Astoria Shanghai on the Bund
■ The Bund

2 Zhongshan No. 1 Road East; tel: 6322 9988; www.waldorfastoriashanghai.com; map p.25 D2; $$$$

The exclusive 1920s Shanghai Club reopened in 2011 as one of Shanghai's premier hotels. Spacious river-view rooms in a new tower complement the 20 deluxe suites in the neoclassical Bund-front building. The star attraction is an update of the Shanghai's Club's legendary Long Bar, while Pelhams and the Grand Brasserie offer magnificent fine dining. Salon de Ville is a chic venue for high tea.

Lap of Luxury

The Ritz-Carton Pudong
■ Pudong
Shanghai IFC, 8 Century Avenue, Pudong;
tel: 2020 1888; www.ritzcarlton.com; map
p.119 G4; $$$$
Reaching for the sky, this hotel
occupies the top 18 floors of the
Shanghai IFC tower. The high-rise
rooms feature contemporary Art Deco
detailing, floor-to-ceiling panoramas
and touchpad room controls. The 58th-
floor Flair restaurant and bar boasts
an uber-hip terrace with great views,
while the 53rd-floor ESPA is a luxury
wellness destination all of its own.

Jumeirah Himalayas Hotel
■ Pudong
1108 Meihua Road, Pudong; tel: 3858 0855;
www.jumeirah.com; map p.119 G3; $$
Incorporated into the eye-catching
Himalayas Art Centre, this cavernous
hotel is themed on modern-meets-
classical Chinese art. The lobby is
dominated by a hand-carved opera
pavilion hosting regular performances,
and all artworks are original. The rooms
have hardwood floors, Ming-style
furnishings and high-end technology.
Among the eateries is J-Mix, a sleek
sushi and teppanyaki restaurant.

The Peninsula Shanghai
■ The Bund
32 Zhongshan No. 1 Road East; tel: 2327
2888; www.peninsula.com; map p.24 D7;
$$$$
The Peninsula Shanghai is the
epitome of classical luxury with
contemporary characteristics. Cutting-
edge in-room technology includes

spa-style music, lighting and humidity
settings, Nespresso machines and a
1,000-channel internet radio. Cocktails
on the riverside at Sir Elly's terrace
are de rigueur, while the spa and
marble layered pool deck could grace
the Great Gatsby movie set. The
Lobby is open for a luxurious high tea
accompanied by a string quartet.

The Langham Xintiandi
Shanghai
■ Xintiandi
99 Madang Road; tel: 2330 2288; www.
xintiandi.langhamhotels.com; map p.48
D3; $$$
In the heart of Xintiandi dining and
shopping district, this elegant luxury
hotel boasts a central location and
superb service. The upper level rooms
afford fine city views. Signature
Cantonese dining is available at
Ming Court and Zen-infused wellness
comes courtesy of the Chuan Spa.

Boutique Stays

Waterhouse at South Bund
█ South Bund

1–3 Maojiayuan Road; tel: 6080 2988; www. waterhouseshanghai.com; map p.49 H3; $$

Created by the owners of Singapore's New Majestic and Town Hall in London's Bethnal Green, this 19-room former warehouse is a hip celebrity bed-down. The highly stylised design features pared-back concrete walls, funky furnishings and outsized art pieces. Each room is individually styled on this 'factory chic' theme. A fourth-floor terrace bar overlooks the Huangpu River, and Table No. 1, created by British chef Jason Atherton, ranks among Shanghai's elite restaurants.

Urbn
█ Jing An

83 Jiaozhou Road; tel: 5153 4600; www. urbnhotels.com; map p.68 B2; $$

Touted as China's first carbon-neutral hotel, Urbn was built using bricks, granite and hardwoods reclaimed from bulldozed local buildings, with intriguing results. The double bed resides in the centre of the room and a sunken mini lounge offers cushioned comfort in a restricted space. Bathrooms feature under-floor heating and rainforest showers. Local celebrity chef David Laris manages the Downstairs restaurant and lounge.

JIA
█ Jing An

931 Nanjing Road West; tel: 6217 9000; www.jiashanghai.com; map p.69 E3; $$

Singaporean entrepreneur, Yenn Wong, waved her design wand on a Nanjing Road heritage mansion and created a Shanghai icon. Funky, playful and exquisitely styled, Jia offers residence-style rooms with quirky furnishings, kitchenettes and an inbuilt ceiling sound system.

Mid-size Chic

Les Suites Orient Bund Shanghai
■ South Bund

1 Jinling Road East; tel: 6320 0888; www.
hotelsuitesorient.com; map p.49 F5; $$
Located on the South Bund,
overlooking the old buildings and
river, this is one of Shanghai's most
sophisticated stays. Decorated in
nutmeg marble and hardwoods,
the rooms feature two TVs, free
smartphone, a window-front rocking
chair, rainforest shower, and free Wifi.
There's also a gym and a guest library
lounge serving tea and refreshments.

The Puli
■ Jing An

1 Changde Road; tel: 3203 9999; www.the
puli.com; map p.68 C1; $$$$
Marketed as an urban resort, this
sophisticated modern hotel blends
Southeast Asian and Chinese design
motifs with fine service and a prime
downtown location. All rooms feature
a free mobile phone, Asian artworks
and glass shutters inset with Jim
Thompson silk. Jing An restaurant
serves up some of the city's most
inventive comfort cuisine, and the
Anantara Spa specialises in wellness
treatments infused with Chinese teas.

Hotel Indigo Shanghai on the Bund
■ South Bund

585 Zhongshan No. 2 Road East; tel: 3302
9999; www.shanghai.hotelindigo.com; map
p.49 F5; $$
Rising 30 floors above the banks of
the Huangpu River, this trendy hotel
stands out for its local art collection
and sweeping city views. Quay 'club
lounge' is open to all guests, offering
a library, iMacs and refreshments.
CHAR Grill and Bar on the 29th and
30th floors has established itself in the
upper echelons of Shanghai dining.

88 Xintiandi
■ Xintiandi

380 Huangpi Road South; tel: 5383 8833;
www.88xintiandi.com; map p.48 B3; $$$
An excellent downtown location and
residential-style facilities makes these
spacious suites a good choice for
business travellers. Each one features
Chinese-infused décor and furnishings,
a lounge with TV and DVD player,
kitchenette and all modern tech
accessories. Some boast balconies
overlooking Xintiandi. Guests can
use the adjacent fitness club, while the
trad-mod styled breakfast dining room
is one of Shanghai's most eye-catching.

Rooms with a View

Park Hyatt
Pudong
100 Century Avenue, Pudong; tel: 6888 1234; shanghai.park.hyatt.com; map p.119 H4; $$$$

Mainland China's highest hotel occupies the 79th-93rd floors of the Shanghai World Financial Centre. Floor-to-ceiling windows offer mesmerising views and Cornerside Park Suites have wraparound vistas – even from the bathtub. The Water's Edge Spa sits beside the swimming pool on the 85th floor and for an extra high, 100 Century Avenue restaurant and lounge spans the top three floors.

JW Marriott
People's Square
399 Nanjing Road West; tel: 5359 4969; www.marriott.com; map p.69 G3; $$$

This pinnacled skytower stands tall over People's Square. All rooms offer great views, plus the requisite modern technology and facilities for a city-centre business hotel. An inset window seat at the 40th-floor JW Lounge is perfect for observing sunset turn into neon-lit nightfall. The Mandara Spa is one of Shanghai's top wellness retreats.

Renaissance Yu Garden Shanghai
Yu Garden
159 Henan Road South; tel: 2321 8888; www.marriott.com; map p.49 E4; $$

The playful contemporary interiors of this modern tower hotel contrast with the dramatic views over the old Chinese city's wing-tipped roofline, which are especially magical at night. Spacious, comfortable rooms, the colourful Quan Spa and a location close to Yu Garden and the Bund are the main draws.

Hyatt on the Bund
Northern Districts
199 Huangpu Road; tel: 6393 1234; www.shanghai.bund.hyatt.com; map p.137 E2; $$

Though a little isolated in the North Bund district, this twin-towered hotel stares directly down the Huangpu River. The vistas, flanked by both the Bund and the Pudong skyline, are magnificent. Pick of the dining options is Xindalu, which serves traditional Peking Duck in a swanky modern setting, while the outdoor terrace and Jacuzzi at Vue lounge is one of Shanghai's most popular destinations for cocktails with a view.

Heart of the Action

Shanghai Marriott City Centre
People's Square

555 Xizang Middle Road; tel: 6279 2213;
www.marriott.com; map p.69 G3; $$

This 720-room business hotel spans
37 floors of a glassy new tower just
north of People's Square. Most of
the downtown attractions are within
walking distance, and Pudong's
business district is a short metro hop.
The contemporary guestrooms are
designed with the busy corporate
traveller in mind, as are the
comprehensive conference facilities
and choice of five restaurants.

Pudong Shangri-La
Pudong

33 Fucheng Road, Pudong; tel: 6882 8888;
www.shangri-la.com; map p.69 G4; $$$$

This long-established luxury giant is a
recognisable landmark on the eastern
bank of the Huangpu River, in touching
distance of Lujiazui's corporate towers
and mega malls. It's class all the way
from the fine French dining at Jade on
36 to Nadaman Japanese restaurant
and the Tibetan-styled CHI Spa.
Choose a river-view room for splendid

panoramas of the Bund – binoculars are
provided.

Four Seasons Shanghai
Jing An

500 Weihai Road; tel: 6256 8888; www.
fourseasons.com/shanghai; map p.69 E2;
$$$$

This high-rise luxury doyen close
to Nanjing Road is not as swanky or
stylish as its brand stablemates, but
the facilities, dining, spa and service
are top class. All rooms are classically
styled and offer all necessary creature
comforts; those higher up the 37-floor
tower offer fine city vistas.

Okura Garden Hotel
French Concession

58 Maoming Road South; tel: 6415
1111; www.gardenhotelshanghai.com;
map p.93 F5; $$

This Japanese-managed hotel
occupies the fabulous 1920s Cercle
Sportif Français Club and a new-build
tower behind. The neoclassical facade
and expansive gardens are sublime.
The hotel is popular with Japanese
guests, and features the excellent
Yamazato restaurant.

Family Friendly

Le Royal Meridien Shanghai

People's Square
789 Nanjing Road East;
tel: 3318 9999; www.starwood.com;
map p.69 H4; $$

With a perfect location overlooking People's Square, this mammoth hotel is within easy walking distance of several kid-friendly attractions, including Madame Tussauds and the Hershey Chocolate museum, as well as other downtown sights. The spectacular Sunday Brunch is a local institution, and kids will appreciate the vast sweet selection. Another plus is the large rooms with floor-to-ceiling windows which give young photographers plenty of scope to snap People's Square's skytowers.

Kerry Hotel Pudong, Shanghai

Pudong
1388 Huamu Road, Pudong;
tel: 6169 8888; www.shangri-la.com;
map p.119 G3; $$

Shangri-La's new luxury business hotel brand dominates the Kerry Parkside complex near Pudong's MagLev station. This vast 574-room hotel features seven floors dedicated to Club accommodation, with 24-hour butlers and Club lounge access. A unique highlight popular with all ages is Kerry Sports, Shanghai's largest hotel-based sports club, which features a 24-hour gym, indoor swimming pool, tennis courts and even a rooftop garden with jogging track.

Value and Comfort

Radisson New World
People's Square
88 Nanjing Road West; tel: 6359 9999; www.radisson.com; map p.69 G4; $$

Impossible to miss due to its UFO-like rooftop restaurant, this comfortable modern hotel offers spacious rooms with satellite TV and high-tech facilities right in the heart of Shanghai. There's a spa, virtual golf simulator, gym and swimming pool, and the spaceship restaurant actually rotates – albeit very slowly. Great fun.

Old House Inn
French Concession
No 16, Lane 351, Huashan Road; tel: 6248 6118; www.oldhouse.cn; map p.92 C4; $

Tucked away down an old lane, this small homely abode is designed in 1930s Shanghai style, with four-poster beds, traditional Chinese furnishings and Art Deco lamps. The creaking hardwood floorboards echo a pleasing sense of French Concession history. Breakfast is served in the delightful Purple Onion restaurant in the leafy walled courtyard.

Baolong Home
Jing An
125 Nanyang Road; tel: 5174 8188; www.bljj.net.cn; map p.68 C2; $

Centrally located one block from central Nanjing Road, this small hotel is designed like a traditional Chinese courtyard home, with grey bricks, granite floors and sepia photographs of Shanghai scenes. The 66 basic single and double rooms are relatively small, but comfortably furnished with free Wi-fi, TV, rainforest shower and air conditioning. A good option for cost-conscious visitors seeking a hint of local style.

Astor House
Northern Districts
15 Huangpu Road; tel: 6324 3179; www.pujianghotel.com; map p.137 D2; $

Located just a few minutes from the Bund, across Suzhou Creek, this 1910 gem was once Shanghai's top hotel. The interiors have been spared large-scale gentrification and much of the original detailing remains, albeit a little rough around the edges. A mix of basic accommodation and more refined suites are available. Breakfast is served in the historic Peacock Hall, once the city's smartest ballroom.

Essentials

A

Addresses

In most modern buildings, the ground floor is 1/F. Buildings are sequentially numbered, odd numbers on one side of the street and even numbers on the other. Because the major streets often run the entire length of the city, it helps to know what the nearest cross-street is when trying to locate an address, such as Nanjing Road West near *(kaojing)* Maoming Road.

B

Business cards

In business and other formal situations in Shanghai, you will be expected to present a business card. Present cards with both hands, and accept them the same way.

C

Children

Shanghai loves children. There is not a museum, a restaurant or a theatre where your child will feel unwelcome. Hotels often allow children to stay with parents in a double room at no extra charge. Extra beds are available for a small surcharge. Reliable babysitters, known as *ayi* (aunty), are easily available.

Climate

Shanghai has a northern sub-tropical monsoon climate with four distinct seasons. Rainfall is plentiful throughout the year, though most of it falls during the rainy season from June to September. Expect hot and muggy summers with temperatures hovering in the mid-30s°C (95°F) in July and August, and chilled-to-the-bone damp winters in December and January. January is the coldest month, although temperatures rarely dip below zero. Snow is rare in Shanghai, although there are the occasional late December/January flurries. Shanghai's mildest weather (and best times to visit) is in spring (mid-March to May) and autumn (September to early November).

Clothing

Shanghai errs on the side of casual, but it is a city of unrelenting style: you'll be forgiven for not wearing a tie, but never for looking like a bumpkin. Light, breathable clothes work best in the hot, humid summertime, with a light wrap for the over-air-conditioned restaurants and offices. In winter, several layers of clothing is the key to staying warm, as buildings are sometimes under-heated.

Consulates

Australian Consulate: 22/F, CITIC Square, 1168 Nanjing Road West; tel: 5292 5500; www.china.embassy.gov.au
British Consulate: Suite 301, Shanghai Centre, 1376 Nanjing Road West; tel: 6279 7650; www.uk.cn
New Zealand Consulate: 1605–1607A,

989 Changle Road; tel: 5407 5858; www.nzembassy.com

Singapore Consulate: 89 Wanshan Road; tel: 6278 5566; www.mfa.gov.sg/shanghai

United States Consulate: 1469 Huaihai Middle Road; tel: 6433 6880; also American Citizen Services: 8/F, Westgate Mall, 1038 Nanjing Road West; tel: 3217 4650, after-hours emergencies tel: 6433 3936; http://shanghai.usconsulate.gov.

Crime and Safety

Shanghai is a relatively safe city, but petty crimes like pickpocketing do occur in crowded areas like train stations, markets and on busy streets. There is very little violent crime against foreigners, but tourists should be aware of scams. It's a safe city for women, too, who are able to walk alone, even at night, without being harassed – but again, you should be on your guard.

Customs

Duty-free allowance per adult is as follows: two bottles of liquor (75cl each), 400 cigarettes. There is no limit to the amount of foreign currency and Chinese renminbi (RMB) traveller's cheques that can be brought in; the unspent portion may be taken out. There is a long list of prohibited items, including animals, firearms, plant material and media deemed 'detrimental' to China's social and political security. For up-to-date

details see www.china.org.cn. Note: antiques require a government stamp in order to be exported; most reputable dealers can take care of the necessary paperwork.

D

Disabled Travellers

Most of Shanghai's modern hotels, buildings and museums are all wheelchair-accessible, but older buildings and the myriad overpasses and underpasses are not. Newer metro stations all have wheelchair ramps or lifts, and the older ones are adding them. Bashi Taxi (tel: 6431 2788) has several minivans that cater for the wheelchair-bound.

E

Electricity

Shanghai's electrical system runs at 200/220 volts and 50 cycles AC. Sockets take Australian-style three-pin triangular plugs or circular two-pins. Chinese-to-foreign conversion accessories – whether conversion plugs or voltage converters – are easily available at department stores and hotels.

Emergency Numbers

Public Security Bureau: 710 Hankou Road; tel: 6321 5380
Ambulance: 120
Fire: 119
Police: 110

F

Further Reading

Rise of a Hungry Nation: China Shakes the World, James Kynge (2006). This excellent book by a former *Financial Times* Beijing bureau chief explains all you ever needed to know about the factors behind, and social consequences of, China's economic rise.

New Shanghai Cuisine (2005), Jereme Leung. Executive chef at the Whampoa Club takes a historical, and beautifully photographed, journey through the complex cuisine of Shanghai.

Life & Death in Shanghai, Nien Cheng (1987). Harrowing autobiographical tale, written in exile, about incarceration and survival during the Cultural Revolution;

Western Architecture in Shanghai: A Last Look, Tess Johnston and Deke Erh (2004). Beautifully photographed book chronicling the origins and architects of Shanghai's rich portfolio of western-influenced villas, mansions and historic houses.

Carl Crow – A Tough Old China Hand, Paul French (2006). Fascinating story of an intriguing character – an American journalist, ad-man and social networker – who became an intrinsic feature of 1920s/1930s Shanghai.

In Search of Old Shanghai, Lynn Pan (1982). Historical musings about old Shanghai by probably the city's best chronicler.

Empire of the Sun (1984), JG Ballard. This emotive wartime story of a young boy interned by the occupying Japanese would later became a major movie.

Shanghai Baby, Wei Hui (2002). Controversial sex, drugs and bad girl memoir that somehow came to define late 1990s Shanghai.

H

Health

No vaccinations are required to enter Hong Kong, but doctors often recommend immunisations against flu, tetanus and Hepatitis A & B. Tap water should be boiled before drinking and bottled water is widely available. For current information on influenza and other health concerns, see www.who.int/csr/en.

Medical Services
Healthcare is good in Shanghai, and improving all the time. There are Western-staffed clinics and designated foreigners' clinics in local hospitals with English-speaking personnel. For more serious and complicated issues, patients often return to their home countries or seek treatment in Hong Kong. Similarly, all the medication you might need – over-the-counter and prescription – should be brought with you, as not all medication can be found in Shanghai.

Hospitals and Clinics
Shanghai Huashan Hospital

Foreigner's Ward; 19/F, 12 Wulumuqi Middle Road; tel: 6248 9999 ext 1900. A mid-sized general hospital which offers most specialities except obstetrics and gynaecology, and paediatrics.

Pudong Children's Medical Centre; 1678 Dongfang Road, Pudong; tel: 5873 2020. A large, modern teaching hospital built as a Sino-US joint venture.

Ruijin Hospital; 197 Ruijin No. 2 Road; tel: 6437 0045, ext 8101 (outpatients and emergencies only); 6324 0090 ext 2101 (24-hour house calls). Large teaching hospital. The foreigners' clinic is located in Guang Ci Hospital, in the grounds.

Parkway Health, Shanghai Centre Clinic; Suite 203, West Retail Plaza, Shanghai Centre, 1376 Nanjing Road West; tel: 6445 5999; www.parkwayhealth.cn. Reputable clinic with overseas-trained and English-speaking doctors and staff. Operates clinics throughout the city. For 24-hour assistance, call 6445 5999.

Pharmacies
Parkway Health centres will fill prescriptions (*see above*).

Shanghai No. 1 Dispensary; 616 Nanjing Road East; tel: 6322 4567; daily 9am–10pm.

Watsons; 789 Huaihai Middle Road; tel: 6474 4775; daily 9am–10pm. Branches all over the city.

Holidays

New Year's Day: 1 Jan
Spring Festival: Jan/Feb*
Qing Ming: Apr*
Labour Day: 1 May
Dragon Boat Festival: June*
Mid-Autumn Festival: Sept/Oct*
National Day: 1 Oct

Note that Spring Festival (or Chinese New Year) and National Day are often week-long holidays. Schools and government offices are open the weekend before or after the one-week holiday. Spring Festival and National Day holidays signal a huge migration of travellers across China, and trains, airlines and hotels are booked out well in advance. (*denotes holidays determined by the lunar calendar)

Hours

Offices open Monday to Friday 9am–6pm. Government offices are open 9am–5pm during weekdays with a 1–2-hour lunch break. Banks may stay open until 6 or 7pm; some currency exchange desks are open around the clock, and ATMs are everywhere.

Most large malls and department stores open from 10am–10pm, seven days a week. Smaller shops may have shorter hours. Keep in mind that most businesses are closed during Chinese New Year and other national holidays.

I

ID

Visitors should carry with them a form of photo identification, such as passport, or a photocopy of it at all times.

Internet

Most business hotels either have in-room Wi-fi or broadband access. There are wireless cafés all over the city as well.

L

Language

Shanghai's official language is Mandarin (Putonghua). Local residents also converse in the Shanghainese dialect. English is increasingly understood by the younger generations in cental areas (though not by taxi drivers so always have your destinations written in characters). Street names, public transport and utilities signage is written in Chinese and Pinyin (phonetic) or English translation, as are many restaurant menus.

M

Maps

Free tourist maps of Shanghai in English and Chinese are available at the airport and from most hotels. The maps sold at the bookshops are usually in Chinese. Recommended is the *Insight Fleximap Shanghai*, laminated for durability.

Media

Newspapers and Magazines

Shanghai Daily (www.shanghaidaily. com) and Beijing-based *China Daily* (www.chinadaily.com) are both published in English. Foreign newspapers and publications are available from the city's four- and five-star hotels. One of the best sources is The Portman Ritz-Carlton Shanghai, which carries the *South China Morning Post*, *International Herald Tribune*, *Asian Wall Street Journal* and magazines like *Economist*, *Time* and *Newsweek*.

Shanghai is awash with free English-language publications of varying quality, most with useful listings of restaurants, bars and entertainment spots. Among the best are *Time Out* (www.timeoutshanghai. com) and *City Weekend* (www.city weekend.com.cn).

Radio

BBC World Service is accessible on radio. English-language programming is on FM 101.7 and FM 103.7.

Television

Shanghai has two English language channels. News and cultural programmes are broadcast on China Central Television (CCTV) Channel 9, while ICS is a locally produced channel with slightly more entertaining programming, including foreign movies. Most hotels offer a range of international cable and satellite channels.

Money

The Chinese yuan (CNY) is also known as renminbi (RMB). One yuan or renminbi (colloquially called *kuai*) is divided into 10 jiao (colloquially known as *mao*); one jiao is divided into 10 fen. RMB bills are issued by the Bank of China in the following denominations: one, five, 10, 50 and 100. Coins come in denominations of one kuai, and 50, 10 and five fen.

Changing Money

Exchange rates are uniform regardless of whether you change money at a bank or hotel. Major currencies can be changed at hotels (but you must be a registered guest) as well as at banks. The same applies for traveller's cheques. Slightly better exchange rates are offered for traveller's cheques as opposed to cash.

Credit Cards and ATMs

International credit cards and bankcards (Cirrus, Plus, Visa, MasterCard, American Express) can be used to withdraw local currency from ATMs, which are found throughout the city. International credit cards are now accepted at major hotels and most restaurants – although many Chinese restaurants and small hotels only take cash or domestic credit cards. Cash is also king in the markets and most smaller local shops.

P

Post

Every neighbourhood in Shanghai city has a post office, recognisable by its dark green and yellow signage. Post offices in the busiest areas, ie Sichuan Road, Huaihai Middle Road,

Nanjing Road and Xujiahui, are open 14 hours, while the Huangpu district post office is open 24 hours. In addition to mailing and selling stamps, post offices also deliver local courier packages. Most large hotels will post letters to international destinations for you.

T

Telephones

The country code for China is 86; the city code for Shanghai is 021. When calling Shanghai from overseas, drop the prefix zero. When making a domestic call from one province to another in China, dial the city code first (including the prefix zero). Local calls within Shanghai do not require the city code. To make an international direct dial call from Shanghai, dial the international access code 00, followed by the country code, the area code and the local telephone number.
Local directory assistance: 114
International operator: 116

Most public telephones in China use prepaid phone cards, which can be used for local, long distance and international (IDD) calls. Prepaid phone cards are available in amounts of RMB20, 30, 50 and 100.

Mobile (Cell) Phones

To avoid roaming charges, get a pre paid SIM card with a local number and fixed number of minutes. Many phone providers, hotels, convenience stores and self-serve kiosks at airports sell them in denominations of RMB100. Calls are charged by the minute. The main service providers are Shanghai Telecom, Shanghai Mobile and China Unicom.

Time
Shanghai (and all of China) is on Beijing time, which is 8 hours ahead of Greenwich Mean Time (GMT).

Tipping
Locals do not generally tip and it is not usually expected. For taxis and many restaurants, you needn't tip, but in international restaurants it is becoming accepted. RMB 10 per day is reasonable for a tour guide. Hotels and some high-end restaurants add a 15 per cent service charge to bills automatically.

Tourist Information
A tourist hotline (tel: 962 020) operates daily from 10am to 9pm. Information can be patchy depending on who you get on the line. Be sure to ask for an operator who speaks English. **The Shanghai Tourist Information and Service Centre** (http://lyw.sh.gov. cn/en) operates branches in each of Shanghai's districts, including one on the ground level of the arrival hall of Pudong International Airport, though these are geared towards Chinese-speaking travellers. Hotel concierges in five-star hotels and local tourist magazines and websites are generally the best source of current information.

City Weekend (www.cityweekend.com. cn) has a useful text messaging service that sends addresses in Chinese to your mobile phone.

Transport
Shanghai has an efficient, easy-to-use and well-priced transport system.

Arriving by Air
Shanghai has two airports (www. shairport.com): **Pudong International Airport** (30km east of the city centre – code PVG) is mainly for international flights. **Hongqiao Airport** (15km west of the city – SHA) is for domestic flights and some Hong Kong, Taiwan and South Korean routes. Getting from both airports to the city is straightforward. **From Pudong**: official taxis into the city cost RMB80–150, depending on your destination. The MagLev train (one way RMB40 with same-day air ticket, return RMB80) links with Longyang Road metro station (metro line 2) in Pudong – from here, catch a metro or taxi to your onward destination. Eight air-conditioned airport bus routes transport passengers around the city (RMB18–30, route details are posted in the arrivals hall). **From Hongqiao**: The Hongqiao Transport Hub connects Terminal 2 with metro lines 2 and 10, Hongqiao Railway Station and the long-distance bus station. Terminal 1 connects with metro line 10 only. Taxis are easily available and cost between RMB20–100 to downtown, depending on destination.

Getting Around

Bus: Shanghai's bus system can be confusing for visitors and bus routes in Chinese characters. Taxis, which are very cheap, or the metro are better options.

Metro: Thanks to a pre-Expo 2010 infrastructure boom, Shanghai has the longest metro system in the world. Shanghai currently has 11 metro lines (with several more under construction) running all across the city from around 6am to midnight. Everything is signposted in English and Chinese, and on-train stop announcements are multi-lingual. Metro line 2 connects Pudong International Airport in the east with Hongqiao Airport in the far west.

Taxis: Taxis are easy to hail on the street, outside rush hours – Dazhong (96822) and Jingjiang (96961) are reputable companies. Fares are cheap and always metered, and receipts are given if requested. Flag fall is RMB13 (RMB15 after 11pm) for the first 3km, and RMB2.4 per km thereafter. Tipping is not expected.

V

Visas

Most visitors to China require a visa. There are several ways of procuring one. The easiest way is to use the services of a travel agent. There will be a commission charge on top of the visa-processing fee paid to the visa office of the Chinese embassy or consulate. Individual travellers may also apply for a visa directly with the Chinese embassy or consulate in their home country. Two passport-size photos, the completed application form and the fee are required. It takes about 7–10 working days to process your China visa, so make sure you apply for one well before your intended departure.

W

Websites

The following websites provide a variety of information on travel-related subjects on Shanghai.

General Information
www.china.org.cn

China Foreign Ministry
www.fmprc.gov.cn/eng

Shanghai Government
www.shanghai.gov.cn
www.investment.gov.cn

Health Matters
www.worldlink-shanghai.com

Banks in Shanghai
www.sbacn.org

Airport Information
www.shanghaiairport.com

Government Travel Services
www.cits.net
www.ctsho.com
www.cnto.org
www.cnta.gov.cn

Entertainment and Events
www.cityweekend.com.cn
www.timeoutshanghai.com
www.smartshanghai.com

Hotel Bookings
www.ctrip.com
www.elong.com.

Index

Insight Select Guide: Shanghai
Written by: Amy Fabris-Shi
Edited by: Cathy Muscat and Tom Le Bas
Layout by: Ian Spick
Maps: Apa Cartography Department
Picture Manager: Steven Lawrence
Series Editor: Carine Tracanelli

Photography: AJL Photography Ltd 7B, 37
Alamy 40/41, 65, 81, 86, 89, 94, 98, 101, 102, 103,
105, 111, 114, 125, 139, 147, 151, 156, 157, 160, 161,
162, 163; Art Labor Gallery 113; Astor House
179B; Jason Atherton 60; Shreyans Bhansali 63;
Corbis 140; Chris Cypert 122; Fairmont Hotel
172T; Four Seasons 177T; Getty Images 30, 53,
88, 112, 146; Hazara 132; Himalyas Hotel 129 ;
Indigo Shanghai 175T; Chee Hong 110; Istock-
photo 4/5, 17; Photolibrary 104, 116, 120/121,
134, 148, 159; Derryck Menere Photography
172B; Le Royal Meridian 3T, 178;
PA Photos 15, 29, 43, 64, 74, 141; Park Hyatt
176; Peninsula Hotel 173; Pudong Shangri La;
The Puli 175B; Radisson Blu New World 179T;
APA Ryan Pyle 2, 9, 10/11, 12, 13, 14, 31, 33, 36,
42, 44/45, 50, 54/55, 56, 57, 58/59, 61, 62, 70, 72,
77, 80, 82/83, 87, 90, 96/97, 124, 126, 127, 128,
144/145, 150, 164, 167; Andrew Rowat 85; APA
David Shen Kai 3B, 6B, 6T, 7T, 8, 9, 16, 19, 22,
26, 28, 32, 34, 35, 38, 39, 46, 51, 52, 66, 73, 75, 76,
78/79, 84, 95, 99, 106/107, 108, 109, 115, 123, 128,
130, 131, 133, 138, 142/143, 152, 158, 168, 169;
Urban Hotel 174T; Waterhouse Bund Hotel
174B; Scott Wright 149

First Edition 2012
© 2012 Apa Publications UK Ltd.
Printed in Germany

Distribution:
Distributed in the UK and Ireland by:
Dorling Kindersley Ltd
(a Penguin Group company)
80 Strand, London, WC2R 0RL, UK
email: customerservice@dk.com

Distributed in the United States by:
Ingram Publisher Services
1 Ingram Boulevard, PO Box 3006, La Vergne,
TN 37086-1986; email: customer.service@
ingrampublisherservices.com

Distributed in Australia by:
Universal Publishers
PO Box 307, St Leonards NSW 1590
email: sales@universalpublishers.com.au

Worldwide distribution by:
Apa Publications GmbH & Co. Verlag KG,
(Singapore Branch), 7030 Ang Mo Kio Avenue
5, 08-65 Northstar @ AMK, Singapore 569880
email: apasin@singnet.com.sg

Contacting the Editors
We would appreciate it if readers would alert
us to outdated information by writing to:
Apa Publications, PO Box 7910, London SE1
1WE, UK; email: insight@apaguide.co.uk

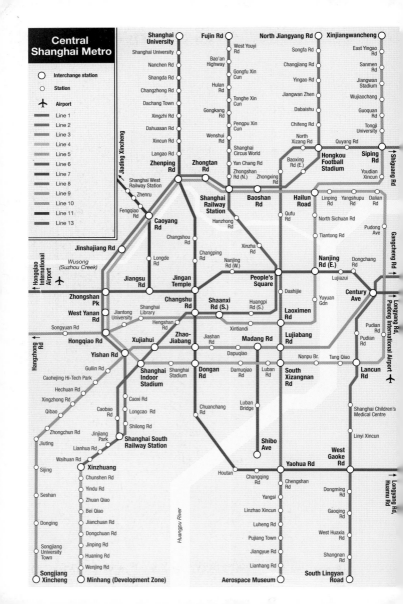